Ages 2-3 Teacher Guide

Year Red, Semester 1

By Kathleen Lull Seaton (Core) and Lisa Marquart Riensche (Bonus)

This teacher guide accompanies the Ages 2-3 Learner Resource and the Age 2–Grade 4 Teacher Class Kit.

Bible Backgrounds: Janet M. Corpus and Sarah S. Henrich
Editors: Barbara S. Wilson, Julie Lindesmith, and Carolyn F. Berge
Designer: Carl Nelson, Chance•Nelson & Associates
Illustrator: Wilkinson Studios
Cover Photos: PhotoDisc

ISBN 0-8066-4703-5

Augsburg Fortress
www.augsburgfortress.org

Witness
Sunday School Curriculum

Contents

Manufactured in U.S.A.
1 2 3 4 5 6 7 8 9 0 1 2 3 4 5 6 7 8 9

Witness

Sunday School Curriculum

Introduction

Welcome to Witness!

Witness Sunday School Curriculum is a great way to teach the kids you know and care about how to "Learn from the Bible to Live the Good News." What is the good news? God promises, provides, and is present throughout human history. God the Father, Son, and Spirit is for us and with us, wherever we are and whatever we do. God is also for others: in our homes, in our neighborhoods, in our churches, and all around the world. That is news worth sharing!

As God's children—young and old, teachers and learners—we are witnesses to God's action in the world. Our salvation story is a story of God's gifts of Word, faith, and service. Each of these gifts functions as both meaningful connection and joyful invitation. **Word** connects us with the biblical story and invites us to use our minds to learn, make good choices, and communicate with others. **Faith** connects us with God's family and invites us to explore and affirm our identity as the church. **Service** connects us with our sisters and brothers, using Jesus as our model, and invites us to act lovingly for them. In Witness, your learners will encounter many ways to witness to others through exploring how they can express their faith in daily life with family, friends, the broader community, and God's creation.

Sunday school teachers play a valuable role in the faith development of young children. Whether you're a teaching veteran or a first-time teacher, this teacher guide will provide what you need to plan and carry out lively, engaging, and meaningful Sunday school sessions for your learners. Witness is designed to support teachers as they prepare for teaching children! Keep reading to learn more about Witness Sunday School Curriculum.

How Should I Get to Know Witness?

First, read pages 2-5 carefully. Then leaf through the Core and Bonus sessions in this teacher guide. Take a look at the leaflets and stickers in the learner resource. Explore the posters, activity cards, and reproducible sheets in the teacher class kit. Listen to the audio CD in the teacher class kit. Get familiar with the abbreviations for the learner resource (LR), teacher guide (TG), and teacher class kit (TCK).

What's in the Teacher Guide?

The teacher guide contains everything you need to know to teach up to 20 Sunday school sessions this semester. In addition to these introductory pages, this teacher guide contains age-level information on page 5, step-by-step plans for teaching 15 Core sessions on pages 6-80, an introduction to Bonus sessions on page 81, step-by-step plans for teaching five Bonus sessions on pages 82-91, and reproducible learner pages for Bonus sessions on pages 92-96. The inside front cover lists the scope and sequence for this semester. A family letter is found on the inside back cover. Make copies of this letter to distribute to learners during the first Sunday school session of the semester.

What's in the Learner Resource?

The learner resource (LR) contains two pages of color stickers and 15 four-page color leaflets to be used during the 15 Core sessions. To reduce week-to-week preparation time, prepare the leaflets and stickers before the semester begins. Separate the nested leaflets and group them by session. Cut apart the stickers and store them by session in small, resealable bags. Use folders or an accordion file to keep the materials for each session separate. Since many session activities require you to show pictures and read directions from the leaflet, make sure you have your own leaflet each week.

What's in the Teacher Class Kit?

Witness teacher class kits (TCK) are terrific for both learners and teachers. They contain posters, activity cards, reproducible sheets, and an audio CD. Many TCK items were designed for use in specific sessions, but some items support teaching and learning throughout the

Learn from th

course. Hang the colorful posters in your class area. Some have a biblical theme and some are designed to help learners make connections with their lives. Use the activity cards to tell stories and teach Faith Traits. Copy reproducible sheets for each learner to use during storytelling, art activities, and games. Among the reproducible sheets in each kit are those used as learner resources for Bonus sessions. Play a track from the audio CD each week and enjoy the varied formats and clever approaches to the Bible stories, using both music and spoken word.

What Are Core Sessions and Bonus Sessions?

There are two types of Witness Sunday school sessions: Core and Bonus. Each semester, the teacher guide contains 15 Core sessions that follow the salvation story. During the first semester of each Witness year, most Core sessions are based on stories from the Old Testament. A few stories at the end of Semester 1 focus on New Testament stories. These stories help learners prepare for Advent and Christmas. During the second semester of each Witness year, all Core sessions have New Testament stories as their basis, most from the Gospels of Luke and Matthew.

Each teacher guide also contains five Bonus sessions for each semester. These sessions offer added variety and flexibility. Read more about the Bonus session format on page 81.

What Is the Format of Each Core Session?

Each Core session is five pages long and describes everything you need for a 60-minute Sunday school session. The first page contains a session-at-a-glance chart that lists estimated activity times, needed materials, and learner activities. Find the Bible Text, the Key Verse, and the kid-friendly Big Idea statement on this page to prepare for presenting the story.

On the second page you'll find the Bible Background, Learner Goals and Age-Level Connection to enrich your preparation. Look for the Teacher Prayer and Question for Reflection in the sidebar for additional support and encouragement. Learner Goals carry out the Witness theme and broaden both teachers' and learners' understanding of the story. These goals match the characteristics of a witness: someone who knows the Word, grows in faith, and shows service. These Learner Goals also carry through to home, because the back page of each leaflet provides ways for families to know, grow, and show. The third, fourth, and fifth pages of each session describe what happens during your time with learners. Two factoids in each session provide additional background about the Bible story. Information about the material you will need and any preparation you should do before class appear as M&P before each activity. Note that activity times on each page are suggestions; expand or shorten depending on your learners' interests, classroom characteristics, availability of materials, and other factors.

Ready for the Story provides ideas for greeting learners and giving them something to do as others arrive, introduces a part of the story through one or more of the senses, and involves all learners in movement. Sidebar items include Witness Words and Transition Tip. Post the Witness Words, teach them during class, include them in word games and puzzles, or use them in other creative ways. Transition Tips help you shift to Explore the Story and may involve movement, signals, or props.

Learners hear the Bible story during **Explore the Story.** Use the Bible art and storytelling script on the second page of the leaflet for Storytelling. After setting up and telling the story, follow the teacher guide's suggestions for discussing the Faith Trait. Sidebar items include Kid Connect and More Movement. Kid Connect helps you engage kids in conversations and activities that are connected to the story. Use the movement activity when learners would enjoy moving their bodies.

Live the Story helps learners apply the story to their own lives and offers ideas for sharing the story and witnessing to others. Creative activity options like Kids Create mean kids can take home original art to help remember the story. Sidebar items on this page include Witnesses in the World, Teacher Boost, and Great Good-Byes. Go Global! is a sidebar in Sessions 2, 6, 9, 12, and 15. Before Session 2 copy Reproducible Sheets S and T (TCK), back to back, for each child. Plan how to use the puzzle with each activity.

Note: Most sidebar items (More Movement, Transition Tip, Witnesses in the World, Go Global!, and Great Good-byes) contain activity suggestions. Because these activities are optional, materials and preparation are not found in the session-at-a-glance chart. Read ahead and plan accordingly!

What Is FAITH Traits?

Faith Traits is an exciting part of Witness that teaches faith-based character and values to kids. Each session relates one Faith Trait to a Bible character and provides one or more activities that develop the trait in learners during the Sunday school session and at home. With the

ble to Live the Good News

inspiration of Bible characters, the guidance of the Spirit, and the support of others in their faith community, Faith Traits strengthen kids to be disciples.

Witness teaches 24 Faith Traits that stem from God's Graces of love, trust, courage, and hope. Love manifests itself as the Faith Traits of generosity, kindness, humility, compassion, empathy, respect, and thankfulness. Trust appears as the Faith Traits of cooperation, loyalty, obedience, boldness, and reverence. Courage shows itself as the Faith Traits of responsibility, self-discipline, perseverance, forgiveness, justice, honesty, and wisdom. Hope shines forth as the Faith Traits of harmony, stewardship, patience, peace, and joy.

Several items in the teacher class kit will help you teach Faith Traits and each session leaflet will include the Faith Trait as well.

How Should I Get Ready for Sunday School?

Find out all you can about your learners—especially what children that age enjoy and how they like to learn. Plan how you will *prepare yourself* to teach each week. Focus on what God's good news means for your life and your learners' lives.

Stock your classroom with basic supplies like paper, markers or crayons, scissors, glue sticks, and tape. Use adhesive putty, tape, or pushpins to display posters from the teacher class kit. Some posters are designed for use during specific sessions; others can be displayed for the entire semester. Make copies of the reproducible pages (TG) and sheets (TCK) as you need them so that you have the correct number. The more you do ahead of time, the more time you will have to chat with kids as they arrive.

What Kind of Space Do I Need to Teach Witness?

Witness sessions can be used in a traditional classroom space with a table and chairs. Many activities encourage the use of comfortable spaces for storytelling and open spaces for movement. Pillows, beanbags, and other soft seating arrangements encourage learners to relax and enjoy stories. Carpet squares give each child a defined space when sitting in rows or a circle. When playing games that involve lots of movement, remove obstacles to make sure your learning space is safe.

How Can I Connect with My Learners?

Develop a warm relationship with each learner to build a positive foundation for learning and teaching in your Sunday school group. Use these tips throughout the semester to connect with your learners and help them feel important and valued in the group and loved by God.

- Learn each child's name and use names often during each session. Name tags help, especially when class sizes are larger or when some learners do not attend regularly.
- Welcome each child each week. Sit or kneel so you are at eye-level. Ask questions about activities, pets, family members, and other people and things important to kids.
- Encourage peer relationships! Use name tags and play name games to help learners remember their peers' names. Plan cooperative activities so everyone works toward one goal. Pay attention to how learners connect with each other in pairs, small groups, and all-boy or all-girl groups, and use the groupings that work.
- Provide alternative ways to participate when activities ask for hugging, since some kids are uncomfortable with this type of touching. Handshakes, high fives, and pats on the shoulder may be preferred.
- Ask learners to help with group tasks such as passing out leaflets, pressing the CD player button to start a song, and collecting art materials. Offer enthusiastic and genuine thanks for their help.
- Use the SOS (Some Other Stuff) activities on Reproducible Sheet H (TCK) when you have extra time in the classroom.
- Create consistency in Sunday school sessions so learners know when activities begin and end. You might use a chime or bell to signal a change to the next activity, or flip the lights on and off.
- Pray for your learners and the teaching ministry in your congregation.

Learn from the Bible to L

Age-Level Characteristics

Nurturing faith in Sunday school involves building relationships and understanding kids. Age is one of the biggest factors in determining how kids will learn and act. Here are some general traits of two- and three-year-old learners, some ideas for building relationships in your classroom, and a few tips for sharing God's good news in kid-friendly ways.

Two- and three-year-old kids:

- Are always learning.
- Have short attention spans, are energetic, and are constantly in motion.
- Exhibit developing large muscle and fine motor skills.
- Enjoy playing side-by-side.
- Revel in music and dance.
- May experience separation anxiety.
- Are curious, creative, and often spontaneous in their actions.
- Learn through their senses, by doing rather than observing.
- Are proud of their accomplishments.
- Are learning to take turns and share.
- Can follow simple directions, but vary in their verbal skills.
- Prefer to sit on the floor, rather than in chairs.
- Need to experience love.
- Like to share stories about themselves, their families, and their friends.
- Need physical contact with people and things and enjoy tactile experiences.
- Respond imaginatively to storytelling.
- Enjoy listening to stories and looking at illustrations.

To nurture faith and build relationships with these kids:

- Use their names often.
- Celebrate birthdays or baptismal anniversaries.
- Ask them about their lives each week and listen carefully to what they say.
- Praise their accomplishments but also provide unconditional love and acceptance.
- Provide a safe place for them to share their stories.
- Have fun together; be a friend.
- Provide a safe physical environment and a predictable classroom routine.
- Enlist their help with passing out materials, cleaning up, and turning out the lights.

Use these strategies to develop friendships between kids:

- Say their names often.
- Plan activities where kids can play together, or side-by-side.
- Provide toys for them to share.
- Take time each session for kids to share what's happening in their lives.

To help them learn from the Bible to live the good news:

- Show them where the stories are in the Bible.
- Invite them to be story characters in dress-up clothes and dramatize the story.
- Have them search for toys, puppets, or other story props you have hidden around the room, and then use them to tell the story.
- Dig into a Bible story with activities that tap different skills and interests, such as cooking, exploring outside, playing games, going on treasure hunts, or completing puzzles.
- Tell echo stories and sing echo songs; use rhythm, music, and dance to involve kids in the story.
- Invite them to respond to a Bible story with art—painting, drawing, or clay sculpture.
- Get cozy and read Bible storybooks together.
- Provide blocks and other creative building materials.
- Pray before eating.
- Communicate with caregivers about what's happening in Sunday school, and encourage kids to share Bible stories at home.
- Be "Witnesses in the World" and do service projects that will benefit kids and others in your congregation, community, and the world.

the Good News

A Final Word

As a Sunday school teacher, you share the Word, express your faith, and serve God and others. At Augsburg Fortress, Publishers, everyone involved in the writing and production of Witness sincerely hopes that these materials meet your teaching needs and help you and your learners travel further on your faith journeys. God bless you and your learners!

God Made the World

1

Bible Text

Genesis 1; 2:1-3

Key Verse

God saw everything that he had made, and indeed, it was very good. Genesis 1:31

BIG Idea

God created the world because God loves us.

LR = Learner Resource
TCK = Teacher Class Kit
M&P = Materials and Preparation

Session at a Glance	What You Need	What Learners Do
Ready for the Story (15 minutes)		
Welcome the Witnesses	• Toys and books, tag board, scissors, hole punch, yarn, blue and green markers	• Explore the Sunday school room and make name tags.
Take a Look	• Playdough, globe	• Experiment with play-dough to make ball shapes.
Try This	• Light switch	• Distinguish between dark and light, night and day.
Explore the Story (15 minutes)		
Story Set-Up	• Leaflet 1 (LR), crayons	• Examine some things God created.
Storytelling	• Bible, Poster A (TCK), small table, Bible, Leaflet 1 (LR), CD player, Witness CD (TCK), items from the natural world	• Add to the creation story background.
I Can Too: Faith Traits	• Mirror; Reproducible Sheets A and B (TCK), scissors, stapler, Sticker Sheet 1 (LR)	• Learn about God's love for each of them and make Faith Traits booklets.
Live the Story (30 minutes)		
Ways to Witness	• Plants, small watering can, water	• Discover how to help care for God's creation.
Kids Create	• Witness CD (TCK), CD player; construction paper, magazine pictures, glue sticks • Playdough, small paper plates, nature items (twigs, pinecones, shells, nuts, feathers), marker	• Create a nature collage. • Create a nature stabile.
Worship Together	• Bible, copies of the family letter (inside back cover)	• Thank God for making the world and people.

Bible Background

What Factors Shaped This Story?

Genesis is a poetic expression of belief that God created the world for good, for joy, and for interdependent relationships. The date and author of this writing are hidden in the long, rich history of Israel's life with God. The message is not intended to provide a scientific explanation of how creation happened or how everything works. Rather, the message speaks powerfully of the who and why of creation—celebrating God's good action on behalf of this world, our home.

What Is This Story About?

Genesis praises God's creation. Creation is the awesome home for all of the works of God's hands, including people, designed for their well-being. Genesis also is full of thanksgiving. Not only has God created all of this intricate beauty, but God has created us, too, as remarkable, wonderful creatures. Humans are called to be in charge of God's creatures. God has given us a remarkable vocation: to be stewards, partners with God in the ongoing preservation of creation. In those roles we participate in what sustains, blesses, and increases the glory of God's handiwork. The command "Love your neighbor" is about taking such good care that all of God's creatures flourish.

Why Is This Story Important?

The story of creation reminds us with whom and through whom we begin. A measure of the joy that creation inspires in us comes from knowing that its beauty has a source far beyond us. Its size, its complexities, and its interconnections leave us awestruck. The power of God's creating word challenges both our hearts and our minds to recognize the wonder of human beings as well. At their best these final creations show signs of the love and strength that God wills for all of life. Can we rise to the challenge of living in accordance with God's will?

Age-Level Connection

Young children are familiar with many of the objects named in the creation story. In this session the learners have opportunities to connect their experiences in the world with God. They hear that God made the world for us to explore and enjoy because God loves us.

Teacher Prayer

Creator God, what a wonderful and diverse world you have made. You created plants, animals, and people, but also colors, tastes, and smells. Help me to guide the learners to notice and acknowledge the many signs of your great love surrounding us. Amen

Question for Reflection

What aspects of creation are not mentioned in the Bible story? Consider God's creative designing of seasons, temperatures, textures, and sounds.

Learner Goals

KNOW
that God made the world

GROW
in their understanding that God loves them

SHOW
a way that they can care for the world

FACTOID

The Jewish day began at sundown, so a full day was measured from evening to evening.

Ready for the Story (15 minutes)

Witness WORDS

God, world, Bible

Welcome the Witnesses

M&P *Examine the toys, materials, and books you have available, including the class area itself. If needed, gather items that are appropriate and interesting for use by two- and three-year-olds. Cut a 6" (15 cm) circle from tag board for each child, punch a hole at the top of each circle, and tie a 24" (60 cm) piece of yarn through for a name tag. Have blue and green markers or crayons out.*

Greet the children by name as they enter and invite them to look around the room. Young learners may need help in separating from parents. Try offering a specific toy or book to each child. If you have very young learners, you may want to encourage adults to stay with the children for at least part of this session. Print each child's name on a circle name tag. Provide blue and green markers for coloring the circles to look like the earth.

Take a Look

M&P *Purchase playdough or make it using this recipe: Combine 2 cups (500 ml) flour, 1 cup (250 ml) salt, and 4 teaspoons (20 ml) cream of tartar in a saucepan. Stir in 2 cups (500 ml) cold water mixed with 4 tablespoons (60 ml) oil and several drops of food coloring. Cook over medium heat, stirring constantly until a ball forms. Store in a covered container. Have a globe available.*

This may be some children's first church school experience. Help the children make a circle by holding hands and then sit down. Go around the circle and say hello to each child by name. Encourage learners to wave to each new friend.

When the children are settled and comfortable, offer each a lump of playdough. **What can you do with the dough?** Encourage poking, pulling, and manipulating the dough. Demonstrate how to roll the dough in your hands to make a ball. Repeat this process with the children. **What does the dough look like when it is rolled into a ball?** *(A ball, an apple, the world.)* Show the children the globe. **This is what our world looks like from space. See how the globe has a round, ball shape. Does anyone know who made the world?** *(God.)* **God made the world for us. The world is a wonderful place to live.** Collect the play dough.

FACTOID

Ancient people feared the darkness and welcomed each new day as a reminder of God's victory over the dark chaos at creation.

Try This

Gather together on the floor. **Before God made the world, everything was dark and empty.** Explain that you are going to turn the lights off, and then do so. **In the beginning the world was dark and empty and lonely. Then, God made the light.** Turn the lights back on and invite the children to clap for the light. **God called the dark "night" and the light "day."** Turn the lights off and have the children name the dark, "night." Turn the lights on and together, call the light, "day." **What do we do at night?** *(We go to bed. We sleep.)* Encourage the children to pretend that they are sleeping when the light is off and wake up when the light is on.

Transition Tip

Put away toys and other distractions during the storytelling. Have several adults available for the story. Two- and three-year-olds are better listeners when they are able to sit on a lap or next to a friendly adult.

Explore the Story (15 minutes)

Story Set-Up

M&P *Have available Leaflet 1 from the Ages 2-3 Learner Resource (LR) and crayons.*
Distribute the leaflets. **Look at the front page. What do you see? Some things are colored. Which things aren't?** *(Tree, sun, fish, bird, cow, and child.)* **God made all these things. God made colors too.** Suggest that the children use crayons to color the picture. **Where have you seen these items?** Help the children name other things God made. **Today's Bible story today is about things God made.**

Storytelling

M&P *Display Poster A from the Ages 2–Grade 4 Teacher Class Kit (TCK) at the children's eye level. Place a small table beneath the poster. Have available a Bible, Leaflet 1, a CD player, and the Witness CD (TCK). Gather familiar items that God made, such as a stone, a shell, leaves, fruit, and toy animals, and people figures—enough so that each learner has one.*
Hold up the Bible. **This is a very important book. What is it?** *(The Bible.)* **The Bible tells us about God.** Show learners the beginning pages. **The very beginning of the Bible, Genesis, tells us that God made the world.** Give each child one of the objects. Read the story printed inside the leaflet, having learners put their items on the table. Then listen to Track 1, "Creation Bounce," on the Witness CD.

I Can Too: FAITH|Traits

M&P *Copy Reproducible Sheets A and B (TCK), back to back, for each child. Cut along the horizontal lines, then fold and nest the pages in order and staple to make a booklet. Cut the Session 1 sticker from each Sticker Sheet 1 (LR). Have available an unbreakable mirror.*
God made such a huge, wonderful world! It's a big gift to us. The Faith Trait for today is a big word: generosity. God is so generous to us. Would you like to see the most wonderful thing God made? Let each learner look into the mirror. **Who do you see? God planned for the world to have men and women, boys and girls, and little babies. God planned for people to be the best creation of all, because God loves us.** Hand out the "Little Book of Faith Traits" booklets you assembled and Generosity stickers. Help learners attach the stickers on page 1 and print their names on the front. Collect the booklets. You will use them each session.

Introduce the song "Spread the Good News." Sing it to the tune of the first two lines of "Twinkle, Twinkle."

God loves me. Oh, God loves me.
Spread the good news: God loves me.

Kid Connect

The children in the class may not be familiar with each other. Point to each child in the group and say his or her name: **God made ____. God loves ___.**

More Movement

Stand up and try singing "Spread the Good News" using stanzas such as "God made eyes" or "God made toes." Have the children use fingers to bend and stretch in order to touch each body part named.

Teacher Boost

What aspect of creation is of particular importance to you? Do you have a favorite project, plant, or pet that you could bring into the classroom for the children to examine?

Witnesses in the World

Collect pictures of many different geographic features of the world such as oceans, mountains, and deserts. Display these pictures so that the learners are able to examine the great diversity of God's creation.

GREAT good byes

If the children are willing, give each of them a hug as they leave. Say to each child: **I am glad that God made you, ______.**

Live the Story (30 minutes)

Ways to Witness

M&P *Bring several potted plants, a watering can, and water to class.* Gather the children around the plants. **Here is something else that God made. What is it?** *(Plants, flowers.)* **God wants us to take care of the things that God made. How can we care for the plants?** *(Give the plants water and sun. Be gentle with the leaves and flowers.)* **We can show love for the plants God made by taking good care of them.** Give each learner an opportunity to water one or more of the plants. **When we care for the things God made, we remember that God gave us good things because God loves us.**

Kids Create

M&P *Creation Collage: Collect construction paper, glue sticks, and pictures of things God created. Have the CD player and Witness CD out. Creation Collection: Collect items such as twigs, pinecones, nuts, leaves, and flowers. Small paper plates, a marker, and playdough, as well as the CD player and Witness CD, are also needed.*

Creation Collage: God's world is all around us. Demonstrate how to use the glue stick to attach pictures of things that God made to sheets of construction paper. **Look at the pictures and name the things you see that God made. Then choose pictures that you like and glue them to the paper.** As they work, talk with the kids about the pictures they chose. Help the children name more things that God made as you print "God Created" on their collages. Play CD Track 17, "Creature Sounds," as children work.

Creation Collection: Young children enjoy handling all kinds of natural items. Show the learners how they can select items and press them into a lump of playdough on a paper plate. **Have you ever seen these items near your homes? Can you name these things God made?** Print "From God's World" on each plate. Play CD Track 17, "Creature Sounds," as children work.

Worship Together

M&P *Have available a Bible and items to go home. Photocopy the family letter on the inside back cover of this guide.*

Gather together for a few quiet minutes. Repeat the song "Spread the Good News" from page 9 and add stanzas such as, "God made Mom," "God made trees," and "God made love." Open the Bible to Genesis 1:31 and read the key verse for this session: **God saw everything he had made, and it was very good.** Try saying the words together. Show the children how to fold hands for prayer as you read the prayer on the back of the leaflet. Have children respond, "And it was very good." Collect name tags. Send home Leaflet 1, the family letter, and projects the children made.

Noah and the Flood

Session at a Glance	What You Need	What Learners Do
Ready for the Story (15 minutes)		
Welcome the Witnesses	• A variety of blocks for building	• Play with blocks and use them to build boats.
Take a Look	• Playdough and animal cookie cutters	• Explore animal variety by making some from dough.
Try This	• Rain clothing (raincoat, hat, boots, umbrella)	• Explore concepts of wet and dry, here and far away.
Explore the Story (15 minutes)		
Story Set-Up	• Leaflet 2 (LR), Sticker Sheet 2 (LR), crayons	• Discover what God asked Noah to build.
Storytelling	• Poster A (TCK), small table, Leaflet 2 (LR), CD player, Witness CD (TCK), toy animals, Bible	• Hear the story of Noah and the flood.
I Can Too: Faith Traits	• "Little Book of Faith Traits" booklets (Session 1), Sticker Sheet 1 (LR)	• Play the game "Teacher Says" and add to their booklets.
Live the Story (30 minutes)		
Ways to Witness	• Pinecones or cardboard tubes, yarn, vegetable shortening, craft sticks, birdseed, shallow pan, sandwich bags, scissors	• Make bird feeders.
Kids Create	• Graham crackers, animal crackers, vanilla icing, craft sticks	• Create an ark snack.
	• Marker, large sheet of paper or poster board, glue sticks, small squares of red, orange, yellow, green, blue, and purple paper	• Make a rainbow.
Worship Together	• Bible, Poster A (TCK) or Rainbow Mosaic	• Thank God for caring for us.

2

Bible Text

Genesis 6–9

Key Verse

God remembered Noah and all the wild animals and all the domestic animals that were with him in the ark. Genesis 8:1a

BIG Idea

God keeps promises to us.

LR = Learner Resource
TCK = Teacher Class Kit
M&P = Materials and Preparation

Teacher Prayer

Heavenly Father, how great is your love for your children! Even when we fail to keep our promises to you, you continue to show love and mercy. Forgive our sinfulness and increase our desire to live as your family on earth. Amen

Question for Reflection

What are some of the ways that we can live faithfully amid the chaos and sinfulness of our world today?

Learner Goals

KNOW
the story of God's love for Noah and the animals

GROW
in their knowledge that God promises to love us always

SHOW
concern for animals in our world

FACTOID

The ark would have been approximately the length of one-and-a-half football fields.

Bible Background

What Factors Shaped This Story?

This richly packed and important text is made up of two ancient traditions woven into three episodes. Each episode has its own themes (6:5—7:12; 7:13—8:19; 8:20—9:17), all of which turn around the pivotal verse 8:1. God had willed a creation ordered around stewardship and Sabbath rest, but creation resisted its creator and betrayed God's purposes. From 6:5—7:24 God is seriously grieved by the creation. The evil heart of humankind (6:5) troubles the heart of God (6:6). This text suggests that there is a painful crisis for God in God's dealings with creation. By the end of this passage there is a change in God, rather than in humankind, which gives the opportunity for a new beginning for creation itself.

What Is This Story About?

In this story, Noah will be a sign of future possibilities. He alone is not at odds with his creator. The turning point of the story comes in 8:1, where God "remembered Noah" and all the creatures with him. God's remembering leads to a new beginning for creation. Fresh from the ark, Noah worships God at a newly built altar. God speaks in his heart (8:21), the very place where God had been troubled. God makes a vow based on his own decision and character, for God recognized that the human heart has not changed and will not. Hope for creation can be based only on God's patient love. Humans will betray their creator, but God will and does still keep promises. This promise to sustain creation even when its creatures resist God's love is good news for Noah and for us.

Why Is This Story Important?

In 9:1-7 we hear again words from the first creation story. Humans remain in God's image. They are still to be fruitful. But now God is deeply aware of human weakness (8:21). Grace is God's willingness to try again with us. Everyone who is a loving parent, or had a loving parent, might understand the hope and vulnerability of love like God's. In Genesis, the creator of the cosmos expresses such love in the promise to never again destroy all of creation by flood. Christians see God's vulnerable love and God's power over destruction in the saving events of Jesus' death and resurrection.

Age-Level Connection

The story of Noah is a favorite among young children. The building of the boat and the gathering of the animals are familiar themes for two- and three-year-olds. The children are not ready to grasp what happened in the flood nor the vast mercy of God's love for Noah. However, they are able to hear that God promised to care for Noah and for them.

Ready for the Story (15 minutes)

Welcome the Witnesses

M&P *Gather a variety of building materials such as wooden blocks, cardboard blocks, and plastic bricks.*
Greet each learner by name. Invite the children to come and see the blocks you gathered. Give the children time to build with the blocks. With young learners it is helpful to sit on the floor with them to encourage and include everyone. Suggest that the children try building boats. **Today's Bible story is about an amazing boat built long, long ago.**

Take a Look

M&P *Have playdough and animal cookie cutters available. See the playdough recipe on page 8.*
Offer each child a lump of playdough. Demonstrate how to flatten the dough with hands. Give the children animal cookie cutters to press into the dough. Name the animals that the learners make. Roll the dough back into balls, flatten again, and cut out another animal. Encourage the children to share and take turns with the cookie cutters. **What other animals can you name? Listen and look for some of them in today's Bible story.** Point out that animals can live in many places such as houses, farms, jungles, and in zoos.

Try This

M&P *Bring in rain gear such as a raincoat, rain hat, boots, and an umbrella.*
Gather the children together. Hold hands, make a circle, and sit down. Take a look outdoors and notice the weather. **Is it sunny or rainy? Is it wet or dry? What happens when it rains?** *(We get wet. We need to find ways to stay dry. We stay inside.)* **What can we use to stay dry in the rain?** Offer the learners the opportunity to try on different types of rain gear. With your help, give everyone a turn with the umbrella. **In the Bible story today God told Noah what he needed to do to stay dry during a big rainstorm.**

Witness WORDS

Noah, ark, flood, rainbow

FACTOID

During the flood, not only did water fall from the sky as rain, it gushed out of the ground like a geyser!

Transition Tip

Establish a comfortable place for storytelling near a bulletin board or wall where you can display the story posters. Add a rug or carpet squares.

Explore the Story (15 minutes)

Story Set-Up

M&P *Have Leaflet 2 from the Ages 2-3 Learner Resource (LR), hearts from Sticker Sheet 2 (LR), and crayons available.*

Direct the learners' attention to the front of the leaflet. Introduce Noah to the children. **What is Noah holding in his hand?** *(A hammer.)* **The Bible tells us that God loved Noah. God asked Noah to build something from wood. What do you think Noah made? Use your crayon to follow the dots to see what God wanted Noah to build.** Offer help where needed. **Who knows what Noah built?** *(A boat, an ark.)* **In the Bible this boat is called an ark. God told Noah that a very big rainstorm was coming. The boat would help Noah, his family, and some animals stay dry.** Find out more about love inside the leaflet, and add heart stickers.

Kid Connect

Storms can be unsettling to children. Look for opportunities to remind the learners that God promises to keep them safe. God planned for parents, teachers, and other adults to watch over children when they are worried or frightened.

Storytelling

M&P *Display Poster A (TCK). Place a small table below the poster to serve as Noah's ark. Have available a leaflet, a CD player, the Witness CD (TCK), a Bible, and a variety of toy or stuffed animals.*

Distribute the toy animals that you gathered. Point out the picture of the story of Noah's Ark of Poster A. **You can use these animals to help tell the story.** Hold up the Bible and remind the learners that the Bible tells us about God and God's people. Open the Bible to Genesis 6. Read the story inside of the leaflet, making certain to name all the animals that the children have. Give each learner an opportunity to place his or her animal in the "ark." Play CD Track 17, "Creature Sounds," in the background and enjoy the animal accompaniment. You may also play Track 2, "Extreme Quarters!" and talk about the narration. **Noah loved and obeyed God. God kept Noah and the animals safe and dry during the flood.**

More Movement

Invite the children to pretend that they are animals entering the ark. Try walking in the style of different animals such as swinging trunks like elephants, waddling like ducks, hopping like frogs, and crawling like snakes. Encourage the learners to suggest other animals and movements.

I Can Too: FAITH Traits

M&P *Locate the "Little Book of Faith Traits" booklets from Session 1 (page 9) and each Session 2 sticker from Sticker Sheet 1 (LR).*

The Faith Trait for today is obedience. Who obeyed God in the story? *(Noah.)* **God asked Noah to do several things. What did God ask Noah to build?** *(An ark.)* **What did God ask Noah to take with him in the ark?** *(All kinds of animals.)* **Did Noah do what God asked him to do?** *(Yes.)* **Noah obeyed God. Noah did what God asked him to do.** Hand out each "Little Book of Faith Traits" booklet and the Session 2 sticker. Help learners attach the stickers to page 2 and read the activity ideas. Collect the booklets.

Let's play an obedience game to practice doing what we are asked to do. Have the learners stand. Use the phrase "Teacher says…" to give simple directions such as touching toes, clapping hands, hopping, or turning around. **We obey our parents and teachers. We can obey God, too, just like Noah did.**

Live the Story (30 minutes)

Ways to Witness

M&P *Have available pinecones or cardboard tubes, yarn, vegetable shortening, craft sticks, birdseed, a shallow pan, and sandwich bags. You may need a sharp scissors.*

God planned for Noah to care for the animals when it rained. We can care for animals in our world too. Distribute pinecones or cardboard tubes. Tie a piece of yarn to the pinecone or through the tube to create a hanger. Spread vegetable shortening on the pinecone or tube with a craft stick. Gently roll the pine cone or the tube in a shallow pan filled with birdseed. Place in a sandwich bag to send home. **Care for God's creatures by hanging your bird feeder where the birds can come and eat.**

Kids Create

M&P *Graham Cracker Ark: Provide graham crackers, animal crackers, vanilla icing, and craft sticks. Before serving any food, check with caregivers for learners who have food allergies. Provide an alternative, if necessary.*
Rainbow Mosaic: With a black marker, draw a rainbow on a large sheet of paper or poster board. Cut red, orange, yellow, green, blue, and purple construction paper into 2" (5 cm) squares. Have glue sticks available.

Graham Cracker Ark: Noah built an ark and filled it with animals. You can fill something with animals too. Provide each child with a large graham cracker "ark" and several animal crackers. Show the learners how to use icing to glue the animals to the ark. Review the story of Noah as you enjoy eating this snack together.

Rainbow Mosaic: Set the rainbow drawing on a table or the floor with the paper mosaic squares and glue sticks. Encourage the children to name the colors that make up the rainbow strips. **God told Noah that the rainbow was a sign of God's promise. When we see a rainbow in the sky, we remember that God promised never to send a big flood to the earth again.** Display the finished mosaic on a wall or bulletin board.

Worship Together

M&P *Have a Bible available, and Poster A or the Rainbow Mosaic.*
Open the Bible to Genesis 8:1. Read the key verse: **God remembered Noah and all the wild animals and all the domestic animals that were with him in the ark.** Invite the children to repeat it. **God loved Noah and the animals. God kept them safe. When the rain stopped, God gave Noah something beautiful to help him remember God's love and care.** Point to the rainbow in Poster A or the Rainbow Mosaic. **What was it?** *(A rainbow.)* God promises to love and care for us, too. Sing "Spread the Good News," introduced on page 9. Add the stanza, "God cares for me." **Thank you, God, for caring for Noah, the animals, and us.**

Teacher Boost

Bible stories have been handed down from generation to generation. You are another link in the chain that tells the stories of God. Thank God for all the people who have shared these stories.

Witnesses in the World

Young children love to explore the world and view it with wonder. Helping the children connect the rainbow to the promise of God's love may remind them of God's love and care for them.

Go Global!

Read the Go Global! activity on Reproducible Sheets S and T (TCK). See page 3.

GREAT good byes

When it is time to leave, help children gather projects and leaflets. At the door, kneel down and say good-bye to each child. Offer a hug to children who are willing. Say good-bye with: **God promises to care for you, _______.**

Abraham and Sarah

3

Bible Text

Genesis 18:1-15; 21:1-7

Key Verse

The Lord did for Sarah as he had promised. Genesis 21:1b

BIG Idea

God's promises give us hope.

LR = Learner Resource
TCK = Teacher Class Kit
M&P = Materials and Preparation

Session at a Glance	What You Need	What Learners Do
Ready for the Story (15 minutes)		
Welcome the Witnesses	• Table and blanket, pillows, wooden bowls and spoons, Bible-times dress-up clothes	• Play in a tent.
Take a Look	• Wet wipes, biscuit dough, round cookie cutters, cookie sheets, oven	• Make bread.
Try This	• Door	• Play a game of knocking and welcoming.
Explore the Story (15 minutes)		
Story Set-Up	• Leaflet 3 (LR), 4" x 5" (10 cm x 13 cm) fabric pieces, glue sticks	• Add a tent flap to the story picture.
Storytelling	• Poster B (TCK), CD player, Witness CD (TCK), Leaflet 3 (LR)	• Hear the story of Abraham and Sarah.
I Can Too: Faith Traits	• Blanket, Poster B (TCK), "Little Book of Faith Traits" booklets (from Session 1), Sticker Sheet 1 (LR), biscuits, napkins, drinking cups, water	• Wait to be served, serve others, and add to their booklets.
Live the Story (30 minutes)		
Ways to Witness	• Leaflet 3 (LR), crayons	• Identify some people who promise to love them.
Kids Create	• Blue construction paper, glow-in-the-dark star stickers, marker • Construction paper, stickers, crayons	• Make the Promise Sky. • Make Welcome Baby cards.
Worship Together	• Bible	• Thank and praise God.

Bible Background

What Factors Shaped This Story?

Genesis is about God's promise and God's faithfulness to that promise. It also is about how people respond in faith to God's call. People experience this call in the real circumstances of their lives, often in complex and difficult situations. Yet if there is to be a people Israel who will be a blessing to all nations, individuals must discover trust in God who wants and is able to keep those promises. Genesis closes on a note of confidence about God (Genesis 50:20, 24), but it is open-ended. This relationship between God and humans is on a rocky road into God's promised future.

What Is This Story About?

God makes a promise to Abraham in Genesis 12:1-3 and more fully declares it in 17:3-8. God insists that Abraham and Sarah will be parents of a vast number of descendants, even though they are too old for this to be possible. Both Abraham and Sarah have occasion to laugh at the absurdity of it all (17:17; 18:12). Yet they remain willing to receive unknown visitors. In Genesis 18 Abraham takes the lead, hurrying to see to the comfort of his guests, whoever they might be! What Abraham and Sarah receive from them lies at the heart of the passage (18:10, 14). The stranger promises the impossible and asks whether they believe that for God anything is impossible. Can they trust God's impossible promise? Because the stranger knows of Sarah's secret laugh, perhaps he knows other secrets as well, even the secret of God's plan and power.

Why Is This Story Important?

The challenge to trust God's ability to do the impossible in the lives of ordinary people is a recurrent theme in the Bible. It is a central question at the birth of Jesus, when Gabriel reassures Mary that God's promises will be kept. Jesus later tells his disciples that God makes possible the entry of even the most unlikely persons into God's kingdom. Praying in Gethsemane, Jesus gives us another example of trust as he turns his life over to God.

Age-Level Connection

Young children have had experiences with waiting. They wait for parents. They wait for a turn to play with toys. They wait for the arrival of infant siblings or visiting grandparents. In this session the learners hear how Abraham and Sarah waited for a special baby sent from God.

Teacher Prayer

Lord, sometimes your love comes to us in surprising ways! Help me to grow in my ability to trust and believe in you as Sarah did. Keep my heart open to new possibilities and plans you may have in mind for me. Amen

Question for Reflection

What are some ways God has touched your life? Consider the ways that God has given you hope at different points in your life.

Learner Goals

KNOW
that God made and kept a promise to Abraham and Sarah

GROW
in their ability to wait for good things to happen

SHOW
love for new members of the church family

FACTOID

In Hebrew, the word *Isaac* sounds like the word for "laugh."

Ready for the Story (15 minutes)

Witness WORDS

tent, visitors, promise

FACTOID

Both *Sarai* and *Sarah* mean "princess."

Transition Tip

Check with caregivers to discover any food allergies or other sensitivities. Make arrangements to serve foods that the learners may safely eat. Keep a list of allergies posted where all adults working with the class can see it.

Welcome the Witnesses

M&P *Cover a table with a blanket to make a tent. Add some props such as floor pillows, wooden bowls and spoons, and Bible-times clothing items.* Welcome the learners as though they are special visitors. Direct their attention to the tent that you made and invite the children to play inside it. As they explore the items inside, talk about tents. **Have you ever been in a real tent? Have you slept in a tent? Long ago many people lived in tents rather than buildings. Then they could move from place to place.**

Take a Look

M&P *Make biscuit dough or purchase refrigerated biscuit dough. Have round cookie cutters and cookie sheets, and wet wipes for washing hands. Arrange to use an oven. Before serving any food always check with caregivers for learners with allergies. Provide an alternative, if necessary.*

Invite the children to gather around a table. Wash hands or provide wet wipes. Give each child a piece of dough or a prepared refrigerated biscuit. Help flatten the dough. Show how to use a cookie cutter to cut out rounds. Suggest that girls trace *S* and boys *A* on their biscuits. **You will find out what *A* and *S* stand for in the story. In Bible times, people often made round bread to eat. They ate the bread with their families and with people who came to visit. What do you serve people who visit your family?** Bake the biscuits to serve later in the session.

Try This

Sit together on the floor. Have one adult in the group go outside and knock on the door. **Who is knocking on the door?** Have the adult say his or her name. **Hello, ______. Please come in.** Offer the learners the opportunity to knock and tell their names. Welcome each guest who comes to the door. **The Bible story today tells about a time when someone came to visit Abraham and Sarah at the tent where they lived. Abraham and Sarah welcomed the visitors to their home.**

Explore the Story (15 minutes)

Story Set-Up

M&P *Have Leaflet 3 from the Ages 2-3 Learner Resource (LR) out and cut a 4" x 5" (10 cm x 13 cm) piece of fabric for each child. Locate glue sticks.* Distribute copies of Leaflet 3 and look at the front page. **The Bible tells us about the person standing by the tent. Her name is Sarah. Sarah and her husband, Abraham, loved God very much. One day some visitors came to Abraham and Sarah's tent. What do you think happened then? It made Sarah laugh inside the tent.** Give each child a piece of fabric. Glue the top edge to the top of the tent and show how to open the tent to see Sarah.

Kid Connect

What are some times that children need to wait? Do they like waiting? Waiting is hard even for adults. Talk with the learners about how they feel when they have to wait for a parent or a turn to play.

Storytelling

M&P *Have Leaflet 3 available along with a CD player and the Witness CD from the Age 2–Grade 4 Teacher Class Kit (TCK). Display Poster B (TCK).* Look together at Poster B. **In Bible times some people lived in towns. Can you find some buildings? Can you find a well for water? Can you see some rugs? Do you see children? Other people lived far away from towns, in tents.** Hand out the leaflets. **Can you find a rug in the tent?** Read the story and invite learners to respond. **What did God promise to send to Abraham and Sarah?** *(A baby.)* **Do you remember what Sarah did when she heard the promise God made?** *(She laughed.)* Encourage the children to laugh with you. **Sarah laughed because she thought she was too old to have a little baby.** Play Track 3 on the CD, "How the Promise Comes," and sway with the music.

More Movement

Play a waiting game with the learners. Tell them that you would like them to jump, but they need to wait until you say *jump*. Each time you give a direction have the children wait for several seconds. Try touching toes, standing on tiptoe, and hopping.

I Can Too: FAITH Traits

M&P *Display Poster B. Spread a large blanket on the floor, and have the biscuits the kids prepared earlier ready to share. Have water and drinking cups available. Before serving any food, always check with caregivers for learners who have food allergies. Provide an alternative, if necessary. You will need the "Little Book of Faith Traits" booklets (see page 9) and Session 3 sticker from Sticker Sheet 1 (LR) for each child.*

Gather on the blanket. **Today's Faith Trait is patience. Abraham and Sarah had to wait a long time for God's promise to come true, but they were patient. Sometimes they rested in their tent or sat on a rug to wait for God's promise. They ate food and watched what the children around them were doing while they waited for God's promise.** Help learners attach the sticker to page 3 of their booklets, and then set them aside.

Have the children help distribute napkins and the biscuits. Then take another look at Poster B while you wait to eat. **What do you see children doing? Is anyone eating in the scene? It's hard to wait. Abraham and Sarah had to wait a long time for their baby to come.** Say a prayer and enjoy eating together. Explain the *S* or *A* on the biscuits. *(S for Sarah, A for Abraham.)* Provide water to drink.

Teacher Boost

The children are becoming more comfortable with you. The time you spend playing and working with them helps them discover that the church is a place where they are loved and welcome. What a wonderful way to introduce the promises of God.

Witnesses in the World

Recall how Abraham and Sarah welcomed the visitors to their tent. God wants us to be kind and friendly to others. Help the children develop ways of being friendly to the other learners and to guests who come to the class.

GREAT good byes

Say good-bye at the door with a hug or a handshake. **I promise to see you soon. You are my friend.**

Live the Story (30 minutes)

Ways to Witness

M&P *Have the leaflets and crayons available.*

Have learners look inside their leaflets and find the heart. **Who loves you?** Name the people around the heart. **Can you find parents, a grandparent, a pastor, teachers, a doctor, and a friend?** Talk about what these individuals do to care for children. Children can use crayons to draw the lines. **Who else cares for you?**

Kids Create

M&P *Promise Sky: You will need blue construction paper, a black marker, and glow-in-the-dark star stickers.*
Welcome Baby Cards: Provide construction paper, decorative stickers, and crayons.

Promise Sky: The Bible tells us that God promised Abraham more children and grandchildren than there are stars in the sky. What a wonderful promise of a big family. Have the children attach stars to construction paper. Help the learners try to count some of the stars they have attached. On the paper print, "Abraham and Sarah's Children!"

Welcome Baby Cards: How do you think Abraham and Sarah felt when their baby finally came? Do any of you have a new baby at home? It is a wonderful feeling when a baby comes to live with a family. Having a baby can be hard work, but mostly it is a happy time. Everyone wants to welcome a baby and you can too. Make cards by folding a sheet of construction paper in half. Provide crayons and stickers for decorating the cards. On the inside, print, "Welcome, Baby!" Give the cards to the pastor to take to church families who have new babies.

Worship Together

M&P *Have a Bible available.*

When the room is straightened, sit together. Open the Bible to Genesis 21:1b. Read the key verse to the children: **The Lord did for Sarah as he had promised.** Help the children recall what God's promise to Sarah was. **God loved Abraham and Sarah. God promised to send them a baby to love. Abraham and Sarah named the baby Isaac**. Fold hands and thank God for promising to love and care for us. Sing the song "Spread the Good News," introduced on page 9. Add a stanza: "God loves babies."

Baby Moses

Session at a Glance	What You Need	What Learners Do
Ready for the Story (15 minutes)		
Welcome the Witnesses	• Drawing paper, markers	• Name the people who live with them.
Take a Look	• Dishpans or containers, towels, water, dolls, sponges or cloths, plastic cups, smocks	• Wash baby dolls in water.
Try This	• Small doll, blanket	• Look for a hidden baby doll.
Explore the Story (15 minutes)		
Story Set-Up	• Leaflet 4 (LR), Sticker Sheet 2 (LR)	• Hide baby Moses in the grass and learn about helping.
Storytelling	• Bible, Poster C (TCK), CD player, Witness CD (TCK), basket, doll, blanket, Leaflet 4 (LR)	• Hear the story of baby Moses.
I Can Too: Faith Traits	• "Little Book of Faith Traits" booklets (from Session 1), Sticker Sheet 1 (LR)	• Play a game about ways to help and add to their booklets.
Live the Story (30 minutes)		
Ways to Witness	• Toys from the nursery, wet wipes	• Help clean baby toys.
Kids Create	• Small baskets or jewelry boxes, clothespins, small fabric pieces, tape, cotton balls • Poster board, markers	• Make a clothespin Moses. • Make a Helping Hands poster.
Worship Together	• CD player, Witness CD (TCK), Bible	• Thank God for helpers in families.

4

Bible Text

Exodus 2:1-10

Key Verse

His sister stood at a distance,
to see what would happen to him.
Exodus 2:4

BIG Idea

God gives us courage to help others.

LR = Learner Resource
TCK = Teacher Class Kit
M&P = Materials and Preparation

Teacher Prayer

Heavenly Father, you guided Miriam to watch over her brother, Moses. Thank you for all the people who have cared for me over the years. Help me to use my abilities to care for others too. Amen

Question for Reflection

How have you been called to serve God in surprising ways that involved caring for others? Miriam was asked to watch a baby in a basket.

Learner Goals

KNOW
that God took care of baby Moses

GROW
in their understanding that God cares for them too

SHOW
one way that they can help care for a younger child

FACTOID

Levites were one of the tribes of Israel.

Bible Background

What Factors Shaped This Story?

A famine generations earlier in their own land had led the ancient Israelites to Egypt, where they prospered. Though the Israelites had lived in Egypt under favorable conditions, Pharaoh, a new ruler in Egypt, abandoned any hospitality toward the Israelites. Pharaoh feared the power of the Israelite people so he enslaved them. Despite—or perhaps because of—Pharaoh's oppression, the Israelite population continued to grow. Out of fear, Pharaoh ordered that all newborn males among the Hebrew people be killed at birth. Hiding her son was the Levite woman's act of resistance against Pharaoh's edict. The child she saved became the leader of the Israelite liberation.

What Is This Story About?

Though Pharaoh ordered male children killed because he recognized males as a threat to him, in this story it is women who resist Pharaoh's oppressive system. The child's mother saves his life by hiding him. She and the child's sister risk his life, hoping to save it by setting him adrift in a basket on the river. Pharaoh's daughter, having her maid rescue the infant from the river, recognized the child as Israelite or Hebrew, took pity on him, and raised him as her own. Through the intervention of the infant's sister, his own mother served as his wet nurse. It may be because of women's relatively higher status among the ancient Egyptians that Pharaoh's daughter could act so decisively and independently.

Why Is This Story Important?

God's will is accomplished in the events of day-to-day life. The ordinary is a vehicle for the extraordinary. Women, who were not seen to have power, made choices and acted effectively in opposition to the most powerful person around. A Hebrew child who was saved became the liberator of his people. Something important came about through a sequence of simple human events. God's will that people be free is fulfilled in the simple acts of people like you and me.

Age-Level Connection

Young children are proud of the ways that they are growing. However, adults often find it easier and faster to do things for preschoolers. In this session, the learners have opportunities to see themselves as helpers and to participate in caring for others.

Ready for the Story (15 minutes)

Welcome the Witnesses

M&P *Have available drawing paper and markers.*
Be available to greet each of the learners by name, and greet their families too. While family members are still available to help, ask the children to name the people who live in their homes. Make a list for each learner. Label each sheet with, "These are the people who live with _______," adding the child's name. You may refer to the lists later.

Take a Look

M&P *Place dishpans or other containers on a towel-covered surface. Put a small amount of water in each container. Provide smocks for the children to wear. Have dolls, sponges or cloths, and plastic cups.*
Babies usually love water. They like to splash and they like to get clean. Let's wash some babies! Remember to push up sleeves and offer smocks, if they are available. Demonstrate ways to keep the water in the containers. As the children play, talk with them about babies they know. **Who gave you a bath when you were a baby? Do you enjoy taking a bath or playing in the water of a swimming pool?** Comment on the gentle ways the children wash the baby dolls.

Try This

M&P *Wrap a small doll in a blanket.*
Show the children the doll you have wrapped in a blanket. **This baby's name is Moses. The Bible tells us that Moses was a little baby a long time ago. One day Moses' mother hid her baby to keep him safe.** Have the children close their eyes while you hide the baby. Have everyone help look for the hidden doll. Play several times.

Witness WORDS

Moses, sister, helper

FACTOID

Basket, in Hebrew, is *tevah*, a word used in Noah's story to refer to the ark.

Transition Tip

Two- and three-year-olds may wonder why Moses' mother hid her baby. Explain that Moses and his family lived in a place far away from their home. **Moses' mother worried that the people she did not know might try to hurt her baby.**

Kid Connect

Help the children connect the fact that Moses had a family and that they have families too. As you talk and sing together, look for ways to remind the learners that they can care for a brother or sister just like Miriam did.

More Movement

What was it like for Moses to float in a basket on the water of the river? Have the learners pretend that they are sitting in a little boat. Try some actions such as rocking back and forth in the waves, climbing in, and climbing out of the boat.

Explore the Story (15 minutes)

Story Set-Up

M&P *Provide Leaflet 4 from each Ages 2-3 Learner Resource (LR) and the grass, plate, and peanut butter stickers from each Sticker Sheet 2 (LR).* Distribute Leaflet 4 to each child. **Today's Bible story is about a helper. You can be helpers too.** Look at the inside right page and help learners attach the plate and peanut butter stickers. **Look at the front page. Find the baby in the picture. Can you guess what this baby's name is?** *(Moses.)* Give the children the grass sticker to help hide baby Moses. **Moses' mother hid her baby and kept him safe. Moses' sister helped keep him safe too. Now look inside your leaflet. Who is holding the baby and who else is helping? Listen and find out.**

Storytelling

M&P *Display Poster C from the Age 2–Grade 4 Teacher Class Kit (TCK) near the story area and locate a CD player and the Witness CD (TCK). Place a basket under the picture. Wrap a baby doll in a blanket. Have a leaflet out.*
Place the baby doll wrapped in a blanket on your lap. Read the story inside the leaflet. At the appropriate time, place the doll in the basket. Invite the learners to come close and watch baby Moses like his sister, Miriam did. Allow time for the children to share their comments and questions about the story. Point out the picture of the story of Poster C. Listen to "Mo Mo Mo Moses," Track 4 on the Witness CD.

I Can Too: FAITH Traits

M&P *Have available the "Little Book of Faith Traits" booklets (see page 9) and the Session 4 sticker from Sticker Sheet 1 (LR) for each child.*
The Faith Trait for today is responsibility. People who take responsibility for things are good helpers. You can be helpers in your families, just like Miriam. What are some ways you can be responsible and help at home? You may need to suggest ideas such as picking up toys or setting the table. Help each child attach the sticker to page 4 of the booklet. Collect the booklets for use in later sessions.

Stand up and help the children make a circle. Use the tune of the song "Here We Go Round the Mulberry Bush" to sing about ways to help at home using the words, "This is the way. . . ." As you sing each verse, pantomime the actions.

Live the Story (30 minutes)

Ways to Witness

M&P *Gather a variety of plastic toys from the church nursery or other source and a box of wet wipes.*

Everybody can be helpful. Show the children the plastic toys. **Can you think of anyone in the church who might use these? Have any of you ever seen the church nursery? You can help clean the toys that babies use at church.** Distribute wet wipes for washing the toys. As the children wash, talk about why washing toys is a good thing to do. **Toys get dirty and babies like to put thing in their mouths. Washing the toys gets rid of dirt and germs.** Compliment each child for his or her ability to help care for babies in the church.

Kids Create

M&P *Baby Moses: Locate small jewelry boxes or baskets, clothespins, fabric, tape, and cotton balls.*

Helping Hands: Have a sheet of poster board and markers.

Baby Moses: Give each learner a small jewelry box or basket, a clothespin, a piece of fabric, and some cotton balls. **What did Moses' mother do with her baby?** *(Put him in a basket to be safe.)* **What you have could make a basket for baby Moses.** Demonstrate how to wrap the clothespin in the fabric and secure it with tape. Put some soft cotton balls in your "basket" and then the baby. As you work together, encourage the children to tell the story of baby Moses.

Helping Hands: Place a sheet of poster board on a low table. **Look at your hands. What are some ways you can use your hands to help people in your families?** Come up with ideas such as picking objects up, carrying things, turning pages in a book, and giving hugs. **Let's make a poster showing the helping hands of the members of the class.** Invite everyone to add their handprints by tracing around their hands with a marker. Give them time to decorate or color in their hand shapes. Label each hand with the child's or teacher's name. Display the Helping Hands poster where family members can see it.

Worship Together

M&P *Have the CD player, the Witness CD, and a Bible available for worship.*

When the room is straightened and toys and materials are put away, gather together for worship. Open the Bible to Exodus 2. Hold the Bible so that the children can see the words. **The Bible tells us about Moses and Miriam.** Read the key verse for this session: **His sister stood at a distance, to see what would happen to him.** Say the words together. **God cared for Moses and wanted Moses to be safe. God loves us too. God gives us people in our families to love and care for us.** Listen to "Mo Mo Mo Moses" on the CD again.

Teacher Boost

As the children's teacher, you have the opportunity to help them see themselves as capable. This is an important step in nurturing a sense of care and concern within the children.

Witnesses in the World

How does your congregation care for babies and children in the area and around the world? Provide information to families about donations needed for a food pantry, items collected for children in need, or other projects that families could support.

GREAT good byes

As you say good-bye, offer each learner a sticker. **Thank you, ______, for helping take care of others.** Shake hands or give a hug to each child.

Moses and the Sea

5

Bible Text

Exodus 14:1-30

Key Verse

The Lord…turned the sea into dry land. Exodus 14:21b

BIG Idea

We can trust God when we are scared.

LR = Learner Resource
TCK = Teacher Class Kit
M&P = Materials and Preparation

Session at a Glance	What You Need	What Learners Do
Ready for the Story (15 minutes)		
Welcome the Witnesses	• Black or dark blue construction paper, chalk	• Make stormy day or dark night pictures.
Take a Look	• Dishpans, towels, variety of cups, funnels, bottles, smocks	• Explore what water feels like.
Try This	• Large open space	• Play a chasing game.
Explore the Story (15 minutes)		
Story Set-Up	• Leaflet 5 (LR), blue crayons, Sticker Sheet 2 (LR)	• Color the sea.
Storytelling	• Bible, Leaflet 5 (LR) Poster C (TCK), CD player, Witness CD (TCK)	• Hear the story of Moses and the sea.
I Can Too: Faith Traits	• "Little Book of Faith Traits" booklets (from Session 1), Sticker Sheet 1 (LR), blue towels or large pieces of blue paper	• Play Cross the Sea and add to their booklets.
Live the Story (30 minutes)		
Ways to Witness	• Rhythm instruments, CD player, Witness CD (TCK) or other CD with marching music	• Have a praise parade.
Kids Create	• White paper, crayons, blue watercolors, brushes • Small plastic plates, hole punch, jingle bells, wire twists, stickers, CD player, Witness CD (TCK)	• Make water pictures. • Make tambourines.
Worship Together	• Bible, Leaflet 5 (LR)	• Thank God for caring for us when we are frightened.

Bible Background

What Factors Shaped This Story?

God called Moses to lead the Israelite people out of slavery. A series of confrontations in which Moses showed the power of God against Pharaoh culminated in a plague of death upon the firstborn sons of Egyptian families. At this, Pharaoh begged Moses and the Israelites to leave. They went out of Egypt and out of slavery. God led them safely into the wilderness toward the Red Sea.

What Is This Story About?

Even the plague of death does not temper Pharaoh's arrogance. He still does not take seriously God's power and sovereignty, so God sets a trap for him. Pharaoh knows the Israelites' weakness and vulnerability wandering in the wilderness and, disregarding the power of God, sends all his military might against a ragtag band of newly freed slaves.

Nor are the Israelites clear about what's going on. Seeing the Egyptians in hot pursuit, already forgetting what God has done, the Israelites blame Moses for the recapture they anticipate. Even Moses doesn't understand. He says that the Lord will fight for them. To which God says, "Why do you cry out to me?" (verse 15). God was with Moses through repeated confrontations with Pharaoh. God is with Moses and the Israelites now. All they need to do is move forward, relying on God's power. God will work with them, in them, and through them.

Moses does as the Lord commands. The waters of the sea part and the Israelites go across on dry land. In the same way, when the Israelites are safely across with the Egyptians in pursuit, the waters return and drown Pharaoh's military—vehicles, army, weapons, and all.

Why Is This Story Important?

The powerful can be arrogant. God stands with the oppressed and wills freedom. Did the waters actually part? Whether they did or not, God's power delivered the Israelites safely from the hands of their oppressor to freedom and a new life. Beside God, the power of this world comes to naught.

Age-Level Connection

Two- and three-year-olds are magical thinkers. They believe that all kinds of events are possible and are likely to find it unremarkable that Moses led the people across the Red Sea. Emphasize that God cared for the people long ago and God cares for us today. When we are frightened, we can ask God to care for us.

Teacher Prayer

Lord, I know that you were with the people of Israel as they left their homes in Egypt. Help me to trust in your care during those times when I am afraid. Give me courage to do what you want me to do. Amen

Question for Reflection

What are some times in your life that you have felt anxious or afraid and how did you sense God's presence with you?

Learner Goals

KNOW
that Moses led God's people across the Red Sea

GROW
in their knowledge that God helps keep them safe

SHOW
that they are thankful for God's love and care

FACTOID

The Israelites' route is uncertain. We know God did not lead them on the most direct route along the coast to their destination but took them a roundabout way (Exodus 13:17-18).

Ready for the Story (15 minutes)

Witness WORDS

Moses, army, sea

FACTOID

Chariots and trained charioteers required technology and wealth. Slavery was one of the costs of maintaining Pharaoh's army.

Transition Tip

After playing a chasing game, the learners are likely to be excited. Walk back to the class area pretending that you are Moses and the people and you must walk a long, long way. Stop and look behind you to see whether the soldiers are following you. **Moses and the people were afraid. They did not want the soldiers to hurt them.**

Welcome the Witnesses

M&P *Locate black or dark blue construction paper and white or yellow chalk for each learner.*

Greet the children warmly by name, and direct their attention to the dark sheets of paper. **Have you ever watched the sky get darker and darker before it rains or when night comes?** Demonstrate how to use chalk to make a stormy-day or dark-night picture. **How do thunder, lightning, and wind make you feel?** As the children draw, talk with them about times that they have been afraid.

Take a Look

M&P *Set up an area for water play with dishpans on towels. Provide smocks. Gather cups, bottles, funnels, and other containers for pouring.*

There's water in today's Bible story. Do you like to play with water? Set out the pans of water and pouring equipment. You might push up sleeves and put on smocks to help keep the learners dry. **How does the water feel? Is it warm or cold? Do you ever go swimming in a pool or a lake? Have you ever been to the ocean?** Help the children recall times that they have been in water and how they felt about being in it.

Try This

M&P *Arrange playtime in a large open space.*

Move to an area where there is space for running, and sit in a circle. **This is a good place for playing a chasing game.** Encourage the children to move quickly to one side of the area while you slowly chase them. Then all move back to the other side of the area and sit down again. **The Bible tells us that there was a time when the people of God were chased by an army of soldiers. The people had to hurry to stay safe. God sent the people a leader to help them. That leader's name was Moses. Do you remember the story of baby Moses? When Moses was older he was able to help God's people.**

Explore the Story (15 minutes)

Story Set-Up

M&P *Have out Leaflet 5 from the Ages 2-3 Learner Resource (LR), blue crayons, and the people stickers from each Sticker Sheet 2 (LR).*
Distribute the leaflets and look at the front page. **What do you see?** *(People, water.)* **The people of God are trying to leave Egypt. They need to cross the sea. Do you see a bridge or a boat?** *(No.)* **The Bible story today will tell us how the people crossed the water.** Have the children use blue crayons to color the sea, and then add the people stickers.

Storytelling

M&P *Display Poster C from the Age 2–Grade 4 Teacher Class Kit (TCK) in the storytelling area. Have a Bible, the leaflets, a CD player, and the Witness CD (TCK) out. Decide which track to play for your learners.*
When everyone is ready, open the Bible to the book of Exodus. **This part of the Bible tells us about Moses and some of the things Moses did when he grew older.** Read the story inside the leaflet. Point to the part of Poster C that illustrates this story and the one about baby Moses. Include time for comments and questions. **God helped the people cross the water. God told Moses what to do to keep the people safe. Moses was a brave leader. Moses and the people trusted God to keep them safe.**

You may want to listen to the narration, " EXIT 14 News: Red Sea Rising" (Track 5 on the CD), or to "Mo Mo Mo Moses" (Track 4) from last time.

I Can Too: FAITH|Traits

M&P *You will need the "Little Book of Faith Traits" booklets (see page 9) and the Session 5 sticker from Sticker Sheet 1 (LR) for each child. Have three blue towels or large pieces of blue paper available.*
The Faith Trait for today is boldness. Moses and the people were bold in the story because they bravely trusted God and walked right through the sea! Hand out the booklets and help each child attach the Boldness sticker to page 5. Talk about the activity suggested and then collect the booklets for use in the next session.

Play a game of crossing the sea. Lay a row of blue towels or sheets of paper on the floor to make the sea. Invite the children to gather on one side of the "sea." Have the learners hold out their hands like Moses. Remove the middle towel or paper and lead the children between the other two. Have the children hold up hands again on the other side as you replace the towel or paper. Play several times.

Kid Connect

God called Moses to be a leader. In this session guide the children to consider some adults who lead them. Talk together about ways that parents, teachers, pastors, doctors, firefighters, and police officers help children know what to do to be safe.

More Movement

Show the children how to play Follow the Leader a new way. Make a circle and have the leader stand inside. Have the leader hop, clap hands, or do another movement. Then invite the learners to follow the leader. Give turns to everyone who would like to be the leader.

Live the Story (30 minutes)

Ways to Witness

M&P *Gather a variety of rhythm instruments. Locate a CD player and the Witness CD or another CD with marching or dancing music.*

When the people of Israel had crossed the sea, they danced and sang. God had kept them safe. They wanted to thank God and show God how happy they were. Invite the children to join you in a praise parade or dance. Distribute rhythm instruments and turn on the CD. Track 18 of the Witness CD has marching music. Move and dance around the room. **Let's pretend we're in a happy parade.** Encourage the children to trade instruments and continue dancing or marching.

Kids Create

M&P *Water Pictures: Have white paper, crayons, blue watercolor paint, and brushes.*

Tambourines: Locate one small plastic plate, two wire twists, several decorative stickers, and two jingle bells for each child. Use a hole punch to punch two holes near the edge of each plate. Set up the CD player with the Witness CD.

Water Pictures: Use crayons to make pictures on white paper. Help the children press as hard as they can to make the colors bright. Most children this age make designs and marks rather than drawings of objects. Affirm all the children's attempts. Show learners how to cover the drawings with blue watercolor paint. As the paint dries, the crayon drawings will show through. **Don't your pictures look like they are under the sea?**

Tambourines: The Bible tells us that God's people had instruments called tambourines to play when they danced and sang. You can make a tambourine to use too. Show the children how to thread a wire twist through a jingle bell and then through a hole in a plate. Twist the ends to secure the bells to the plate. Repeat with a second jingle bell. Stickers could be attached to the plate for decorations. Provide help as needed. Show how to hold the tambourine in one hand and tap lightly with the other hand as you listen to favorite songs on the CD and dance!

Worship Together

M&P *Have a Bible and a leaflet available.*

When the room is picked up, settle everyone in the storytelling area. Open the Bible to Exodus 14:21 and read the key verse: **The Lord turned the sea into dry land.** Try repeating the verse together. **The people of Israel saw how God helped them. They knew that God loved them very much. God promises to love us too.** Fold hands and pray the prayer on the back of the leaflet.

Teacher Boost

You are teaching the children that loving God gives us joy. Look for ways that you and the learners can celebrate God's love, such as singing, dancing, and marching.

Witnesses in the World

What are some of the things that cause people who live near you to be afraid? The members of the class can pray for God's care for people who live where there are storms, floods, or heavy snow. Encourage the children to ask God to help keep everyone safe.

GREAT good byes

Put on the dancing or marching music as you get ready to say good-bye. Invite the children to dance or march to the door to meet parents. Offer a handshake or a hug to each learner. Send home leaflets and projects the children made.

Bread from Heaven

Session at a Glance	What You Need	What Learners Do
Ready for the Story (15 minutes)		
Welcome the Witnesses	• Dishes, pots and pans, toy foods, play stove or cardboard box	• Pretend to prepare food.
Take a Look	• Dishpans, sand, small toy animals and figures	• Play with sand to imagine the desert.
Try This	• Several kinds of bread	• Examine varieties of bread.
Explore the Story (15 minutes)		
Story Set-Up	• Blanket, Poster C (TCK), CD player, Witness CD (TCK), Bible	• Hear a musical version of the Bible story in a comfortable setting.
Storytelling	• Blanket, Leaflet 6 (LR), hole punch, white paper, glue sticks	• Hear the story of the manna and gather manna.
I Can Too: Faith Traits	• Blanket, breads, knife, basket, cups, juice, "Little Book of Faith Traits" booklets (from Session 1), Sticker Sheet 1 (LR)	• Eat a snack thankfully and add to their booklets.
Live the Story (30 minutes)		
Ways to Witness	• Leaflet 6 (LR), crayons, communion wafers or bread	• Investigate foods used at church.
Kids Create	• Cotton balls, construction paper, crayons, glue sticks, marker • Paper lunch bags, glue sticks, food pictures cut from magazines and grocery store ads, food item(s), marker	• Make table tents. • Make collection bags for canned food.
Worship Together	• Bible	• Thank God for the good things God gives us.

6

Bible Text

Exodus 16:1-18

Key Verse

It is the bread that the Lord has given you to eat. Exodus 16:15b

BIG Idea

God gives us what we need.

LR = Learner Resource
TCK = Teacher Class Kit
M&P = Materials and Preparation

Teacher Prayer

Loving God, you have showered us with so many things: homes, clothing, food, places to learn and worship, family, and friends. Help us to remember that we have so much more than we need. Plant the seeds of generosity and sharing in our hearts. Amen

Question for Reflection

Few of us have experienced the anxiety of not knowing from where our next meal would come. Can you imagine the fear and worry of the people of Israel as they wandered in the desert?

Learner Goals

KNOW
that God gave bread to Moses and the people

GROW
in their knowledge that God gives us food to eat

SHOW
thanks for the food that God provides

FACTOID

Moses' brother, Aaron, was with Moses before Pharaoh and in the wilderness. Their sister, Miriam, gifted in music and dance, helped save Moses as an infant.

Bible Background

What Factors Shaped This Story?

Safely out of the hands of their Egyptian captors, the Israelites wander in the wilderness. Recently escaped from slavery and Pharaoh's exploitation, the Israelites have not yet learned a new life of freedom. Accustomed to the ways of imperial Egypt, they do not know how to survive in any other context, much less in the wilderness. Despite God's power that the Israelites witnessed in Egypt and despite God's delivering them safely from Pharaoh's army, the people still cannot imagine themselves as free and under God's care. They complain against Moses because of the hardships of being in the wilderness and they remember Egypt with longing.

What Is This Story About?

Which is more important: food or freedom? The Israelites complain to Moses that they'd be better off in slavery eating bread while the Egyptians eat meat than being free in the wilderness and hungry. The quail and manna God provides for them to eat shows that food and freedom are not traded off against one another. The Israelites gathered manna in the mornings. Some gathered more, some less (verse 17), perhaps because of differing ability based on size, strength, or stamina. When they measured the manna, each had what was needed. Contrary to the distribution of food under Egyptian slavery, God's food in the wilderness provided bread and meat for all according to their need, not too much or too little.

Why Is This Story Important?

When God calls us out of enslavement to new lives of freedom, God does not abandon us to learn new ways on our own. New living takes new learning. New choices teach new discernment. Freedom takes practice. A new way of life is made up of many, many new ways of thinking, doing, and being. Reliance on God's provision along the path that God calls us is how we manage to make our way to a new way of life.

Age-Level Connection

Food is one of the most familiar aspects of the young child's day. Children enjoy talking about and eating a variety of foods. This story, "Bread from Heaven," encourages the learners to think about the food they eat and to acknowledge God's gift of food, in Bible times and now.

Ready for the Story (15 minutes)

Welcome the Witnesses

M&P *Set up an area for pretending to cook and eat. If you do not have play appliances, turn a grocery box upside-down and draw or paint burners on the box to be a stove. Include dishes, pots and pans, and toy foods.*

As you welcome the learners, ask them what good things happened since last time. **Let's pretend to prepare something for the group to eat. How about making juice and sandwiches? What foods do you like to eat with your families?** Encourage conversation about the variety of foods that are available to people. **God made so many different yummy foods for us to enjoy. Isn't it great that God gives us what we need?**

Take a Look

M&P *Fill two or more dishpans or other containers with several inches/centimeters of sand. Gather small toy animals and other plastic figures.*

Show the children the sand boxes you prepared. **What's inside these boxes?** *(Sand.)* **Where else have you seen sand?** *(In an outdoor sandbox, at the beach, in the desert.)* **In the Bible story today, Moses and the people of God were living in a sandy, dry place. Let's pretend that this sand is the place where Moses lived.** Offer toy people and animals to use in the sand boxes for creative play.

Try This

M&P *Ask parents or caregivers to provide different kinds of bread.*

Gather the learners and show them the different kinds of bread. You might include sandwich bread, whole-wheat bread, an Italian loaf, pita bread, and crackers. Have children wash hands and then give them an opportunity to hold and smell samples of the various breads as you name them. **Which of these look familiar to you? Have you tasted them all before? Everyone may have a taste of the breads in a few minutes.**

Witness WORDS

Moses, bread, gift

FACTOID

Moses was basically a meek man and found it difficult to deal with the people's opposition, despite the miracles God performed through him.

Transition Tip

Let the children bring the bread to a table and arrange chairs around the table. Offer the children the opportunity to set the table with napkins and cups at each place.

Kid Connect

There were no stores in the Bible story. There was no food for the people to eat. God loved the people and wanted them to be fed, so God sent them bread. God plans for farmers and other people to grow and make food for us to eat. God loves us too.

More Movement

Have the children lie down on the blanket and pretend to go to sleep. While they rest, gently toss small pieces you cut from coffee filters into the air in another part of the room. "Wake" the learners and suggest that they pretend to take their baskets and go find the bread from heaven just like the people did in the story. Play several times and emphasize that each morning God sent food for the people to eat.

Explore the Story (15 minutes)

Story Set-Up

M&P *Spread a blanket on the floor in the storytelling area and have a Bible with you. Display Poster C (TCK) on a bulletin board or wall. Have Track 6 on the Witness CD (TCK) ready to play on a CD player.*

Sit together on the blanket. Open the Bible to the book of Exodus. Remind the children that this special book tells us about God and God's love for us. **Do you remember any other stories about Moses?** *(Moses as a baby, Moses and the people crossing the sea.)* **The Bible tells us another story about Moses. This is a story about what happened when Moses and the people got to the other side of the sea.** Point out the appropriate story pictures on Poster C.

Play the song "Wand'rin' Far and Wide," Track 6 on the Witness CD.

Storytelling

M&P *Have glue sticks and Leaflet 6 from the Ages 2-3 Learner Resource (LR) available for each child. Use a hole punch to make lots of small white paper circles, 10-15 per learner.*

Still sitting together on the blanket, distribute leaflets and look at the picture on the front. **What do you see?** *(Moses, the people, empty baskets.)* **What did the people have to eat?** *(Nothing.)* Have children use glue sticks to attach the paper circles to the ground on their leaflets. **In the Bible story today God gave food to Moses and the people. Now look inside your leaflet. What is on the ground and in the people's baskets?** Read the story inside the leaflet. Include time for the learners to ask questions or make comments about the story.

I Can Too: FAITH|Traits

M&P *Have the breads examined earlier in a basket cut and ready to eat, with some juice and cups. Set everything on the blanket used since Story Set-Up. Before serving any food, always check with caregivers for learners with food allergies. Provide an alternative, if necessary. Locate the "Little Book of Faith Traits" booklets (see page 9) and the Session 6 sticker from each Sticker Sheet 1 (LR) for each child.*

Today's Faith Trait is thankfulness. The Israelites were thankful to God for giving them food. Help learners add the sticker to page 6 of their booklets as you talk about the activity on that page. Collect the booklets.

What do you see to eat on our blanket? *(A basket of bread.)* Check for clean hands, and then serve bread and juice. **Before we eat let's say thank you to God too.** Say a simple grace with the children such as: **Thank you, God, for the bread and juice. Amen.** Enjoy eating together like the people in the story. As the children eat, talk about what foods they like. **Does your family get food from the grocery store, the market, or a garden?**

Live the Story (30 minutes)

Ways to Witness

M&P *Have out the leaflets and crayons. If possible, have a sample to show of communion wafers or the bread your church uses for the sacrament.*
People eat together at church. Show the children the communion wafer or other bread. **This is a kind of bread that people eat during worship. This bread helps us think about a time that Jesus ate bread with his friends.** Give the children an opportunity to hold the wafer.

Distribute the leaflets and crayons. **Look inside your leaflet and make a communion wafer circle by each picture of a time you eat at church.**

Kids Create

M&P *Manna Reminder: Have a supply of cotton balls, construction paper, crayons, and glue sticks.*
Food Bags: Collect paper lunch bags, glue sticks, pictures of food cut from magazines or grocery store ads, and a marker. Have a can of soup, a box of rice, or other food item(s).
Manna Reminder: It's important to remember to thank God for our food. Does your family say a table grace before meals? Let's make Manna Reminders that you can set on your tables at home. Hand out paper and help learners fold it in half to make table tents. Invite them to decorate their tents with drawings of their favorite foods. Help each child pull a cotton ball apart and glue bits of cotton among the food pictures, to look like manna. Print a reminder of the child's choosing, such as "Thank you, God" or "I Can Pray," on each tent.

Food Bags: Offer each child a paper lunch bag. **What are some things that we could put in this bag?** *(Toys, book, crayons.)* **Usually, people use these bags for food. We can put food in these bags to share with people who are hungry.** Demonstrate putting a can of soup, a box of rice, or other food items in the bag. Glue pictures of food to the outside of your bag to remind you what to do with it. On each bag print the words, "I can share food."

Worship Together

M&P *Have a Bible. Locate the children's completed leaflets and other projects to go home.*
When the projects are complete and the room is cleaned up, sit together in the storytelling area. Open the Bible to Exodus 16:15. Read the key verse to the children: **It is the bread that the Lord has given you to eat.** Mention the Big Idea for this session: **God gives us what we need.** Sing those words quietly to the tune of "The Farmer in the Dell" and have the children join you. Fold hands and give thanks to God for food and all the other things God gives us. Tell children you will look for them next time.

Teacher Boost

Eating together is an important part of what happens in worship and for the fellowship of the church family. The activities you include in the session are helping the children build a foundation for understanding the sacrament of Holy Communion as they grow.

Witnesses in the World

Talk with family members as they arrive about the food bags. Ask each family to fill their bag with foods for your local food pantry. Encourage families to include the children in shopping for food and filling the bag.

Go Global!

Read the Go Global! activity on Reproducible Sheets S and T (TCK). See page 3.

GREAT goodbyes

As family members arrive, invite them into the room. Let the children offer samples of the bread you served. Gather projects, the leaflets, and say good-bye.

Joshua at Jericho

7

Bible Text

Joshua 6:1-20

Key Verse

They raised a great shout, and the wall fell down flat. Joshua 6:20b

BIG Idea

God is with us all the time.

LR = Learner Resource
TCK = Teacher Class Kit
M&P = Materials and Preparation

Session at a Glance	What You Need	What Learners Do
Ready for the Story (15 minutes)		
Welcome the Witnesses	• Puzzles, Activity Card B (TCK), scissors	• Work together to complete puzzles.
Take a Look	• A guest who plays a musical instrument	• Hear the sounds an instrument makes.
Try This	• Empty boxes, tape	• Build a wall with empty cartons.
Explore the Story (15 minutes)		
Story Set-Up	• Leaflet 7 (LR), sponges, shallow containers, brown paint; or 2" (5 cm) squares cut from brown paper bags, glue; or brown crayons	• Make the wall of Jericho.
Storytelling	• Poster B (TCK), Bible, Leaflet 7 (LR), empty boxes from Try This	• Hear and act out the story of Joshua at Jericho.
I Can Too: Faith Traits	• "Little Book of Faith Traits" booklets (from Session 1), Sticker Sheet 1 (LR), Witness CD (TCK), CD player, Leaflet 7 (LR)	• March like the Israelites and add to their booklets.
Live the Story (30 minutes)		
Ways to Witness	• Leaflet 7 (LR), crayons	• Identify some times that God is with them.
Kids Create	• Cardboard tubes, stickers, markers, wax paper, rubber bands, scissors • White paper plates, black crayons, yarn, hole punch, star stickers, yellow and white paper, glue sticks, scissors	• Make trumpets. • Make reminders of God's care.
Worship Together	• Bible, Leaflet 7 (LR)	• Give thanks to God for being with us.

Bible Background

What Factors Shaped This Story?

The Israelites fled Egyptian slavery. God promised to deliver them into a land where they could live as free people. After two generations of wilderness wandering, they were free enough from the ways of slavery and ready for new life in a new land. Historians believe that other tribes, inspired by the story of flight from slavery and by the life of freedom promised by Israel's God, joined those who had fled Egypt. God called Joshua to lead the people into the promised land.

What Is This Story About?

In preparation for the conquest of Jericho, the Lord instructs Joshua what the people are to do. God has determined that the land will be theirs. By marching, blowing horns, and finally shouting, they will conquer the city. Following this seemingly silly plan constitutes people's obedience to God. Though the Israelites had armed men (6:9, 13), the priests are the primary actors, blowing horns and carrying the Ark of the Covenant, sign of God's presence. It is troubling to learn the story that God led one people in conquest of another. Historians speculate that the way of life established by the Israelites in the promised land was, at least at the outset, one of freedom and justice displacing the local systems of exploitation.

Why Is This Story Important?

Is the story literally true? Whatever the facts, the story tells that God kept the promises made to Moses and the people. In partnership with God, God's leaders chosen for the people continued to accomplish what seemed otherwise impossible.

Age-Level Connection

This is an exciting story for two- and three-year-olds. The children will enjoy marching and shouting, but there is another more important aspect to this story. Help the learners make the connection between God's care for the people of Israel and God's love and care for them. The wall of the city fell because God promised to help the people of Israel.

Teacher Prayer

Loving Father, day after day the people of Israel did as you said. They believed that you would be with them as they marched and that you would keep your promise to give them Jericho. Help me to trust in you as I go about my daily routines, whether they are mundane or demanding. Amen

Question for Reflection

Do you know why Rahab and her family were spared? Read her story in the second chapter of Joshua. Rahab risked her life to help the people of Israel.

Learner Goals

KNOW
that God helped the people of Israel

GROW
in their belief that God helps them

SHOW
that they are able to work together

FACTOID

The story of Jericho begins the conquest of Canaan, which the Israelites occupied as the promised land.

Witness WORDS

Joshua, wall, trumpet

FACTOID

Of the adults who set out from Egypt, only two survived to enter the promised land of Canaan 40 years later. One of these was Joshua.

Transition Tip

Give the children sheets of newspaper to cover the table or work area. Other learners could distribute the leaflets and pieces of sponges.

Ready for the Story (15 minutes)

Welcome the Witnesses

M&P *Place a variety of simple puzzles on the floor or a table. Include the story puzzle from Activity Card B from the Age 2–Grade 4 Teacher Class Kit (TCK). Cut the pieces apart and set them out with the Jericho side up.*
Greet the learners by name as they arrive and encourage them to greet each other. Point out the puzzles that you gathered. **Find a friend to work on a puzzle with you. It's fun to work together to get a job done.** Compliment efforts to share and work cooperatively. **You will learn all about these pictures soon.**

Take a Look

M&P *Make arrangements for someone who plays a musical instrument to visit with the children.*
Bring the learners together and introduce your guest. The children will enjoy meeting either an adult musician or a younger member of the parish who is learning to play an instrument. Encourage the guest to tell a little about himself or herself. Have this individual show the children the instrument and then demonstrate how to play it. Perhaps your guest could play a familiar tune such as "Row, Row, Row Your Boat" or "Twinkle, Twinkle, Little Star." Say to the learners: **The Bible story today tells about a time when the people of Israel played trumpets. Something amazing happened when they did it.**

Try This

M&P *Collect 15-20 boxes or cartons. Tape the flaps closed to make large building blocks.*
Direct the children's attention to the boxes that you have collected. **How could we make a wall with these boxes?** Listen to the children's ideas. Build the wall in various arrangements. Encourage efforts to work together. Keep in mind that the process is more important than the product. If the wall falls down, simply build the wall again.

Explore the Story (15 minutes)

Story Set-Up

M&P *Remove Leaflet 7 from each Ages 2-3 Learner Resource (LR). Pour a small amount of brown paint in shallow containers and cut kitchen sponges into 2" (5 cm) squares. If using paint is not an option, cut 2" (7.5 cm) squares from brown paper bags to glue on, or have learners color the blocks with brown crayons.*

Help the children find the picture on the front of the leaflet. **Take a look at the picture and tell me what you see.** *(A city, a town, houses.)* **The Bible tells us that the people who lived in the city of Jericho built a wall around the city. The wall would help keep other people from coming into the city.** Show the children how to use a sponge dipped in paint to complete the wall around the city, glue on paper squares, or color. Give help where it is needed but encourage the learners to do as much as they can.

Storytelling

M&P *Display Poster B from the Age 2–Grade 4 Teacher Class Kit (TCK) in the storytelling area. Have a Bible and a Leaflet 7 available, along with the wall boxes from Try This.*

Gather in the storytelling area and hand out boxes. Point to Poster B. **This poster shows what a city in Bible times might have looked like. What's happening? What are people doing? Can you imagine this city with a wall around it? Stack your blocks in front of the picture to make a wall and be ready to knock it down. It won't be right away, so listen carefully.**

Open the Bible to Joshua 6. **A long time ago the people of God came to the city of Jericho. God talked to Joshua, the leader of the people. This Bible story tells about what God told Joshua and the people to do.** Read the story inside the leaflet and signal when the wall should come down.

I Can Too: FAITH Traits

M&P *Have the "Little Book of Faith Traits" booklets (see page 9) and Session 7 sticker from Sticker Sheet 1 (LR) for each child. Have a leaflet available. Locate a CD player and the Witness CD (TCK) and decide whether you will listen to Track 7 or 18.*

Review the story by listening to the CD Track 7 narration,"Live Action Sports: Crumble at Jericho," or retell the story from a leaflet and play Track 18, "Marching Steps." Once everyone has had enough marching, hand out the "Little Book of Faith Traits" booklets. **God's people marched and marched. They stuck to the plan that God gave them. Today's Faith Trait is perseverance. Someone with perseverance works hard at a job and does what is needed. Joshua and the people showed perseverance.** Help each child attach the Session 7 sticker to page 7 of the booklet. Talk about the activity suggested and then collect the booklets for use next time.

Kid Connect

God expected Joshua and the people to obey. Help the children name some people such as parents, teachers, and caregivers they obey. You may want to suggest situations in which children are asked to obey, such as holding an adult hand to cross the street, playing in kind ways with brothers and sisters, or waiting for a parent while he or she is on the telephone.

More Movement

Try acting out the whole story of Joshua and the wall at Jericho. March six times around the wall the children made. Count each of the times the class circles the wall. On the seventh time have everyone give a loud shout and gently push the wall down. The children may enjoy trying this more than once.

Teacher Boost

Your willingness to spend time with these little ones is teaching them that they are loved and cared for at church. By offering them a variety of activities to match their different interests and learning styles, you show that you value each of them as individuals.

Witnesses in the World

Learn where food is collected in your church or neighborhood. If possible, take the learners to the place to contribute the canned goods they collected over the past week. Giving food to people who are hungry is one way that we obey God, since God wants us to share.

GREAT good byes

Have the children toot on the trumpets they made to say good-bye to each other. Kneel down to the children's level and offer each one a hug or a handshake as they leave.

Live the Story (30 minutes)

Ways to Witness

M&P *Have crayons and each child's leaflet out.*
Help each child open her or his leaflet and find the activity on the right. **God promised to be with Joshua and the people of Israel always, no matter what. Here are some pictures of children. What are these children doing?** *(Waking up, eating breakfast, playing with toys, reading a book, and saying prayers before bed.)* **Draw a line from the clock to each picture of a time God is with you.** Offer the children crayons for drawing lines between the pictures and the clock.

Kids Create

M&P *Trumpets: Collect cardboard tubes, stickers, markers, and rubber bands. Cut a 6" (15 cm) square of wax paper for each child.*
Day and Night Reminders: Gather white paper plates, black crayons, a hole punch, star stickers, and glue sticks. From construction paper, cut out 3" (7.5 cm) yellow suns and white moons. Cut a 12" (30 cm) piece of yarn for each child.

Trumpets: Music helped to bring down the walls of Jericho. Let's make some instruments of our own and see what we can do with them! Offer each child a cardboard tube to decorate with stickers and markers. As the children work, move around the table and enclose one end of the tube with a square of wax paper, held on with a rubber band. Show the children how they can hum or sing into the open end of the tube to make musical sounds. **March in a circle seven times and then blow your horns!**

Day and Night Reminders: Have the children use black crayons to color one half of a paper plate. **Look at your plate and notice that one side looks like the day and one side looks like the night.** On the uncolored side of the plate have the learners glue a construction paper sun. On the dark side offer the children a construction paper moon and several star stickers. Thread a piece of yarn through a hole punched in the plate so that the children may hang the plates up at home. **God cares for us during the day and God cares for us during the night. Hang your plate near your bed to remind you that God cares for you all the time.**

Worship Together

M&P *Have a Bible and Leaflet 7 handy.*
Sit down together in the storytelling area. Open the Bible to Joshua 6:20 and read the key verse: **They raised a great shout, and the wall fell down flat.** Say the words together. Invite the children to join you in giving a loud shout. Pray together the prayer on the back of the leaflet.

God Calls Gideon

Session at a Glance	What You Need	What Learners Do
Ready for the Story (15 minutes)		
Welcome the Witnesses	• Toy farm animals, toy tractor, toy barn (or box)	• Play with a toy farm.
Take a Look	• Scissors, brown paper bags, glue sticks, leaves, masking tape	• Make a tree.
Try This	• Open space	• Play a game with names.
Explore the Story (15 minutes)		
Story Set-Up	• Leaflet 8 (LR), Sticker Sheet 2 (LR)	• Begin to understand God's call and Gideon's farm work.
Storytelling	• White fabric, adult-size bathrobe, guest, undecorated sugar cookies, brick or stone, Leaflet 8 (LR)	• See the story of Gideon.
I Can Too: Faith Traits	• "Little Book of Faith Traits" booklets (from Session 1), Sticker Sheet 1 (LR), undecorated sugar cookies, paper plates, icing, craft sticks, Poster K (TCK), Witness CD (TCK), CD player	• Make a snack for another class, enjoy music, and add to their booklets.
Live the Story (30 minutes)		
Ways to Witness	• Decorated cookies, juice, napkins, cups, guests	• Serve food to guests.
Kids Create	• Reproducible Sheet G (TCK), markers • Blue construction paper, white paint, crayons or markers, wet paper towels	• Make Gideon stained-glass windows. • Make angel handprints.
Worship Together	• Bible, Leaflet 8 (LR), Poster G (TCK)	• Learn about worshiping God.

8

Bible Text

Judges 6:1-24

Key Verse

Peace be to you; do not fear.
Judges 6:23

BIG Idea

God wants us to worship and serve only God.

LR = Learner Resource
TCK = Teacher Class Kit
M&P = Materials and Preparation

Teacher Prayer

Lord, when you sent your angel to Gideon, he wondered why so many things had happened to the people of Israel. Sometimes, I wonder why the world around me is so full of violence and hate. Show me how I can be faithful to you and do your work in the world even when I am discouraged. Amen

Question for Reflection

What is God calling you to do? Consider whether there is a program or need in your congregation or community that you could help.

Learner Goals

KNOW
that God calls people to help others

GROW
in their understanding that the church is a place to worship God

SHOW
that they are able to help others

FACTOID

While the Midianites in this story are enemies of Israel, in Exodus (2:15b-22) Moses lives among the Midianites and marries the daughter of a Midianite priest.

Bible Background

What Factors Shaped This Story?

The book of Judges witnesses to local conflicts over the Israelite settlement of Canaan. Continuing contests over Israelite occupation are the result of the people's disobedience toward God. The establishment of a just and equitable society was not easy. There was conflict among the Israelites and other new settlers as well as with those already on the land. After Joshua's death, God raised up judges to lead the people. The judges included Othniel, Ehud, Deborah, Gideon, and Jephthah. Not until the establishment of kingship in Israel (1 Samuel 8) was there anything like a state or bureaucratic leadership.

What Is This Story About?

Forgetting their deliverance from slavery and the way of life with God that would keep them free, the Israelites turned away from God and became subject to the Midianites. The Israelites struggled to eke out a living. Like those we call guerrilla fighters, the Israelites hid in the "mountains, caves, and strongholds" (6:2). The Midianites routed Israelite settlements, destroying their crops and livestock and ravishing the land itself. When the Israelites cried to the Lord for help, a prophet of the Lord reminded the people of their deliverance from slavery and their unfaithfulness toward the Lord.

A messenger of the Lord went to Gideon, proclaiming that the Lord was with him. Gideon questioned God's presence with the people given all the terrible things that were taking place under the Midianites. Despite the people's disobedience and Gideon's believing that God had abandoned them, the Lord called Gideon to deliver the people.

Why Is This Story Important?

We easily forget God's continuing presence and power in our lives. When we turn away from God and then suffer hardship alone, we blame God for turning away from us. Gideon thinks that God has abandoned the people, when it is the people who have turned their backs on God. Still, despite the people's unfaithfulness and without their repentance, when they cried to God, God called a leader to deliver them.

Age-Level Connection

Young children wonder why they cannot see God or hear God's voice. In this session, they learn that God called Gideon to be a helper. Look for opportunities to guide the children to see ways that God also calls them to love and serve God as they work and play.

Ready for the Story (15 minutes)

Welcome the Witnesses

M&P *Put out farm toys (animals, barn, tractor). If you do not have a toy barn, make one by cutting a door in the side of a cardboard box.*

After you say hello to individual learners, invite them to look at the items you collected. **What do you see here? Where do all of these things come from?** *(A farm.)* Encourage the children to set up and play with the farm toys. **In the Bible story today, a man named Gideon worked on his family's farm.** Encourage the children to share experiences that they have had visiting farms or reading books about farms.

Witness WORDS

Gideon, altar, angel

Take a Look

M&P *Cut open two or more brown paper bags and tape them together to make a long sheet of brown paper, then from it cut out a tree trunk with branches. Gather some leaves that have fallen from trees or cut out some paper leaf shapes. Set out glue sticks.*

There is a big tree in today's Bible story. Direct the learners' attention to the tree trunk you made. **Let's use glue sticks to attach leaves to the branches.** If leaves are falling from trees in your community, talk about the changing seasons. **Gideon sat down to rest under a tree on the farm. Someone came to visit him while he sat under the tree.** Use masking tape to attach the tree to a wall in the storytelling area.

FACTOID

"The angel of the LORD" (Judges 6:11) may be understood to be a messenger of God or as God appearing. In either case, the message is God's own.

Try This

Go to an open space where the children have room to move around. Have the children line up on one side of the space with you opposite them. **When I call your name, come to me.** Then call the children one by one. You may wish to play more than once. Emphasize that the children know their names and come when they are called.

Back in your room, sing the "Spread the Good News" song introduced on page 9, with stanzas added on pages 10, 15, and 20. Sing "God calls me" (a new stanza for today).

Transition Tip

Have learners pretend to "call" each other to a story time and sit down with partners.

Explore the Story (15 minutes)

Story Set-Up

M&P *Have Leaflet 8 from the Ages 2-3 Learner Resource (LR) and the wheat sticker from Sticker Sheet 2 (LR) out for each child.*
Hand out leaflets and look together at the front page. **The man on this page is Gideon. He is a farmer. Gideon is trying very hard to grow food for his family. Gideon is gathering wheat to make flour and bread for his family.** Help the children attach the wheat sticker near Gideon.

Storytelling

M&P *Invite one or more adults to visit. Locate a stone or brick, a piece of white fabric, an adult-size bathrobe, and a leaflet. Have a plate of undecorated sugar cookies, enough for the group and visitor(s). (These cookies will be decorated during the next activity, and served later in the session. Another class will visit later in the session, during Ways to Witness. See page 45.)*
Move to the storytelling area. Place a brick or stone in the middle of the children. Have one adult wear the white fabric as an angel while you put on the robe to play the part of Gideon. **My name is Gideon. One day when I was working on my farm a visitor came to see me.** Take turns with the guest reading the dialogue printed inside the leaflet. When you come to the part of the story about the cakes, place the plate of cookies on the stone or brick. Include time for responses the children may have to the story.

I Can Too: FAITH Traits

M&P *Display Poster K from the Age 2–Grade 4 Teacher Class Kit (TCK) and have the CD player and Witness CD (TCK) available. You will need the "Little Book of Faith Traits" booklets (see page 9) and the Session 8 sticker from Sticker Sheet 1 (LR) for each child. Have the plate of cookies from the previous activity, paper plates, vanilla icing, and craft sticks.*
Gather near Poster K. **Can you find Gideon here? God called Gideon to do something important. And God calls you too. Today's Faith Trait is obedience. Whom did Gideon obey in the story?** *(God.)* **Do you obey God too?** *(Yes.)* Hand out the "Little Book of Faith Traits" booklets and help each child attach the Session 8 sticker to page 8. Talk about the activity suggested and then collect the booklets for use in the next session.

Have all learners wash their hands. **When the angel came to Gideon, he gave the angel food to eat. We can make a snack to share with some friends who come to visit us too.** Move to the table and give each child two or three cookies on a paper plate. Place some vanilla icing on the side of each plate. Show the children how they can use a craft stick to spread the icing on the cookies. Play the song "Giddy-up Gideon," Track 8 on the CD, as the learners work. They will enjoy singing along with the refrain.

Kid Connect

The concept of serving God is complex. It is difficult for small children to think about a relationship with someone they cannot see. In this session you can help the children grasp that we serve God by loving God and other people.

More Movement

The children can continue serving by helping prepare the room for guests. Assign jobs such as covering a table with a cloth, distributing napkins and cups, welcoming the guests at the door, and directing them to the table.

Live the Story (30 minutes)

Ways to Witness

M&P *Arrange for another group of learners to join you for a snack. Before serving any food, check with caregivers for learners who have allergies. Provide an alternative, if necessary. Set out the cookies the children decorated along with juice, cups, and napkins.*

Encourage the children to welcome their guests. Keep the time together short. When everyone is seated, thank God for the food with a simple prayer. **Thank you, God, for juice and cookies. Amen**

Gideon served the angel and we would like to serve you. Give each child a chance to serve someone a cookie. Enjoy eating and talking together.

Kids Create

M&P *Gideon's Stained-Glass Window: Make copies of Reproducible Sheet G (TCK) and set out markers.*

Angel Handprints: Have blue construction paper, white tempera paint, crayons or markers, and wet paper towels.

Gideon Stained-Glass Window: Offer each child a copy of Reproducible Sheet G. **Gideon worshiped God at an altar outdoors. We usually worship God indoors at church. Use markers to make this picture look like a church window. When you see this picture you can remember that any place is a good place to worship God.** Provide markers for coloring.

Angel Handprints: An angel came to Gideon with a message from God. Let's make angel handprints to remind us of Gideon's story. Give each child a sheet of blue construction paper. Gently cover the palm of one hand with white paint and press the hand onto the paper. Offer a wet paper towel for washing hands. Then turn the paper so the fingers point down. Draw a circle for a head at the top of the handprint. Use markers or crayons to add eyes, nose, and mouth. Print on the bottom of the page, "The angel said to Gideon, 'The Lord is with you.'"

Worship Together

M&P *You will need one Leaflet 8, a Bible, and Poster G (TCK).*

Complete clean up and gather for worship. **The angel told Gideon to love God. Gideon worshiped God at an altar outdoors. Churches have an altar indoors.** Point to Poster G. **How are these churches similar to or different from our church?**

One way we show we love God is by listening to stories from God's book, the Bible. Show the Bible, and read the key verse for the session: **Peace be to you; do not fear.** Invite the children to say the words with you. Then pray the prayer on the back of the leaflet.

Teacher Boost

Reflect on how the children felt about having guests. Small children rarely have the opportunity to serve anyone else. The time spent with another class can help the learners experience the good feelings that come from caring for someone else.

Witnesses in the World

What are some ways that your congregation serves other people? If possible, show collections of food, clothing, or other materials. If your church supports a missionary or a mission congregation, display photographs of this person or place. Another possible source of pictures may be the magazine *The Lutheran*.

GREAT good byes

It has been a busy session. Take your time saying good-bye. Thank each child for his or her help in serving the guests. Consider giving each child a thank-you sticker.

Naomi and Ruth

9

Bible Text
Ruth 1

Key Verse
Where you go, I will go.
Ruth 1:16b

BIG Idea
God teaches us to be faithful friends.

LR = Learner Resource
TCK = Teacher Class Kit
M&P = Materials and Preparation

Session at a Glance	What You Need	What Learners Do
Ready for the Story (15 minutes)		
Welcome the Witnesses	• Dollhouse or box, toy furniture, people figures, large toy truck or box	• Move toy families from place to place.
Take a Look	• Small paper plates, craft sticks, masking tape, markers, yarn, glue	• Make happy and sad puppets.
Try This	• Classroom items such as toys, crayons, Bible	• Pretend to move to a new place.
Explore the Story (15 minutes)		
Story Set-Up	• Leaflet 9 (LR), Sticker Sheet 2 (LR), Take a Look puppets, sandpaper, glue	• Make the road Ruth and Naomi travel on.
Storytelling	• Leaflet 9 (LR), Take a Look puppets, Witness CD (TCK), CD player	• Hear the story of Ruth.
I Can Too: Faith Traits	• Poster H (TCK), Leaflet 9 (LR), "Little Book of Faith Traits" booklets (from Session 1), Sticker Sheet 1 (LR)	• Learn the song "God Loves My Family" and add to their booklets.
Live the Story (30 minutes)		
Ways to Witness	• Leaflet 9 (LR), crayons, Reproducible Sheet F (TCK), crayons	• Make love certificates for family members.
Kids Create	• Catalogs or magazines, scissors, construction paper, glue sticks, marker • White paper, stamp pads, fine-tip markers, paper towels	• Make a family collage. • Make a fingerprint family.
Worship Together	• Bible, Poster H (TCK)	• Thank God for families.

Bible Background

What Factors Shaped This Story?

"The days when the judges ruled" (1:1) were difficult. The people who worshiped the Lord were unfaithful, fought among themselves, and experienced oppression from other peoples. Where could faithfulness be found? The story of Ruth is one of faithfulness in a context where women's lives and actions were not usually retold. Women were seen and defined primarily in their relationships to men. Whose daughter, wife, sister, or mother a woman was defined who she was. Family relationships were the basis of identity and entitlement to property and position.

What Is This Story About?

Having married and left their parents' homes, Naomi, Orpah, and Ruth were identified in relationship to their husbands. When the men died, the women faced crises of identity as well as economics. Respectable women were not on their own; how could they remain integrated in the web of social relationships? They could not provide for themselves; in what relationships could they find what they needed? Naomi resolved that each should return to her home. Orpah agreed but Ruth resisted. She remained with Naomi. They returned together to Bethlehem, Naomi and Elimelech's home.

In Bethlehem they were greeted with some astonishment. What will become of them? Perhaps we have a hint of the possibilities in the change from Bethlehem being a place of famine (1:1) to being a place where the barley harvest was about to begin (1:22).

Why Is This Story Important?

Faithfulness to God is realized in our faithfulness to other people. Faithfulness in relationships with other people takes us beyond the boundaries of gender roles, language, nationality, ethnicity, and family status and conventions. Ruth, a Moabite and not born of the people of ancient Israel, bound herself in faithful relationship. Her descendants include ancient Israel's King David and Jesus (Matthew 1:5, 6, 17). The book of Ruth shows that faithfulness takes us beyond the bounds of family conventions. It also shows how intimate, familial relationships can take on historical significance.

Age-Level Connection

Two- and three-year-olds love their families and are beginning to understand that family members make them feel safe in all kinds of situations. In this session the children hear that families help each other in happy and sad times. Activities are included to help children show love for their family members.

Teacher Prayer

Father, there are so many people I have come to love as family members. I thank you for the individuals in my family and those I count as family members. Guide me, like Ruth, to show devotion and love in all my relationships. Amen

Question for Reflection

Is there someone in your life who is like Naomi? Consider how this person came to mean so much to you and whether you have thanked that person for his or her presence in your life.

Learner Goals

KNOW
that Ruth and Naomi loved each other

GROW
in their understanding of families as caring

SHOW
love for the members of their families

FACTOID

Bethlehem means "house of bread." *Elimelech* means "my God is king." *Naomi* means "pleasant." *Mara* means "bitter." *Ruth* means "friendship."

Ready for the Story (15 minutes)

Witness WORDS

Ruth, Naomi, family

Welcome the Witnesses

M&P *Locate a dollhouse or make one from a cardboard box. Have some toy furniture and play figures out. If possible, find a toy truck that will hold the pieces of toy furniture, or cut the flaps from a small box to serve as a moving van.*

Welcome the children and their family members as they arrive today. Show the children the toys that you gathered and suggest that they set up the house. **The people in this house need to move to a new house. Can you help them put their things in the truck?** When the furniture and people are out of the house, move it to another location and have the children help the family move in there. **The Bible story today tells us about a family that moved from one home to another home.**

FACTOID

The Bible explains the Moabites as remote relatives of the Israelites. Moab was the son of Lot, who was Abraham's nephew (Genesis 11:27; 19:37).

Take a Look

M&P *Collect small paper plates, markers, craft sticks, masking tape, and glue. Cut yarn into small pieces. Make a sample puppet.*

Show learners the two sides of the happy and sad puppet you made. **How does this puppet feel?** *(Happy.)* **How about this puppet?** *(Sad.)* **You can make happy and sad puppets too. We'll use them when we hear today's Bible story because both sad and happy things happen in the story.**

Give each child a paper plate, and provide markers for drawing eyes, a nose, and a happy smile on one side and eyes, a nose, and a frown on the other side. Offer help as needed. Some children may also want to glue on small pieces of yarn for hair. When the puppet faces are complete, help each child attach a craft stick near the bottom of the plate for the handle. Add initials and have learners bring their puppets to the storytelling area.

Try This

M&P *Plan where near the class space you could take a walk with the children, and consider having an extra adult or two along. Have small items such as toys, crayons, or a Bible handy for the children to carry.*

The Bible tells us that long ago there was a woman named Ruth. Ruth and her husband's mother, Naomi, decided to move from the place where they lived. They packed their clothing and dishes and food and walked to another place. **Let's pretend to move, too, like Ruth and Naomi.** Give each child something to carry such as a toy, the crayons, or the Bible. Take a walk and then return to the classroom.

Transition Tip

Encourage the children to replace the items that you took with you. Have one or more of the children bring the puppets to the storytelling area.

Explore the Story (15 minutes)

Story Set-Up

M&P *Gather Leaflet 9 from the Ages 2-3 Learner Resource (LR) and the Ruth and Naomi sticker from Sticker Sheet 2 (LR) for each child. Have glue and the happy/sad puppets made earlier available. Cut a 1" (2.5 cm) square of sandpaper for each child.*
Today's Bible story is about a woman named Ruth and her relative, Naomi. Ruth lived with Naomi, Naomi's husband, and Naomi's sons. They were a happy family. Have the children hold up the happy side of their puppets. Name some things that Ruth and her family did together such as cooking and eating, visiting friends, and singing songs. **Then a sad thing happened. Naomi's husband and Naomi's sons died.** Have the children turn their puppets to reveal the sad faces. **Ruth and Naomi were alone. They were so sad. They decided to move to a new place.** Point to the front of the leaflet. Give each learner a piece of sandpaper to glue on the road with the sticker.

Kid Connect

Young children love their families and most of them enjoy talking about the people with whom they live. The configuration of the household makes little difference to small children. Emphasize that God planned for people to live in families. **People in families love and care for each other. God loves all kinds of families—big and small.**

Storytelling

M&P *Have available one Leaflet 9, the happy/sad puppets, a CD player, and the Witness CD from the Age 2–Grade 4 Teacher Class Kit (TCK).* Tell the story as printed inside the leaflet. Have the children use their puppets to show how Ruth and Naomi felt at each part of the story. When you finish, allow time for the children's comments and questions. **Sometimes Ruth and Naomi were sad. Sometimes the women were happy. The Bible tells us that Ruth and Naomi always loved each other. God planned for families to love each other in happy times and in sad times.**

Play the song "I'm Gonna Stick with You," Track 9 on the Witness CD, and encourage learners to move with the music.

More Movement

Say the word *sad* and have the children cover their faces with their hands and look down. Then say the word *happy.* Have the learners jump up, wave their hands over their heads, and cheer. Repeat the sad and happy sequence several times.

I Can Too: FAITH Traits

M&P *Display Poster H (TCK). Have one Leaflet 9 handy. Locate the "Little Book of Faith Traits" booklet (see page 9) and the Session 9 sticker from Sticker Sheet 1 (LR) for each child.*
The Faith Trait for today is loyalty. Ruth loved Naomi and stayed with her; they were loyal friends as well as family members. God wants people to love and care for each other. Point to Poster H. **What are the people on the "Faithful Friends" poster doing?** *(Accept all responses.)* **How can you tell that they are loyal friends?** *(They look happy; they are caring for each other.)* Help learners attach the Session 9 sticker to page 9 of their Faith Traits booklets. Mention the activity on the page and then collect the booklets.

Teach the action rhyme, "God Loves Families," on the back of the leaflet. Encourage the children to say the words and do the actions with you. Describe the members of your family and then ask learners to talk about their families.

Teacher Boost

Not only are you getting to know your learners, but you have opportunities to meet other family members as they bring children and come to pick them up. The time you take to engage these people in conversation helps you become even more familiar with the children.

Witnesses in the World

Ask parents or guardians to bring in photographs of the children's families. Display them at the children's eye level around a red paper heart, on which you have printed "God loves my family." Bring in pictures of your family too.

Go Global!

Read the Go Global! activity on Reproducible Sheets S and T (TCK). See page 3.

GREAT good byes

There are many things to gather up to send home. Have one adult organize leaflets, projects, and coupons. Give each child his or her happy/sad puppet. Encourage children to greet family members with the happy side of the puppet.

Live the Story (30 minutes)

Ways to Witness

M&P *Have out leaflets and crayons. Make copies of the coupons on Reproducible Sheet F (TCK) so that you have two for each child.*
Hand out leaflets and crayons and look inside. **Which children are showing love to others in their families? How can you help and care for members of your families?** Allow time for drawing, and label pictures if appropriate.

Show the learners the coupons you have copied. **The coupons are special surprises for people in your families. The coupon could be for a hug, a kiss, for help with picking up toys, or other kindnesses. While you color your coupons, I'll fill in the name of the person it's for and what you will give.** Acknowledge the many ways that the children can show love for people in their families.

Kids Create

M&P *Family Collage: You will need construction paper, a marker, and glue sticks. Cut pictures of people from magazines and catalogs.*
Fingerprint Families: Cut white paper into pieces about 4½" x 12" (12 cm x 30 cm). Have washable-ink stamp pads, fine-tip markers, and paper towels for cleanup.
Family Collage: Give each child a sheet of construction paper. **Here are pictures of people cut out of magazines and catalogs. Choose pictures to create a family and glue them to the paper. Your collage could look like your family or a family you imagine. Remember that God loves all families.** On each sheet, print "God loves all families." Use this time to talk with children about their families and things they like to do with their families.

Fingerprint Families: Offer each child a sheet of white paper approximately 4½" x 12" (12 cm x 30 cm). Place a child's fingertip on a washable-ink stamp pad and press the finger on the sheet of paper. Make at least one fingerprint for each person in the child's family. Use markers to add features, designs, or a border. While the children work, label the members of each child's family with their names. Label the picture with "God loves my family."

Worship Together

M&P *Have a Bible and Poster H (TCK) available.*
Gather in the storytelling area. Open the Bible to Ruth 1:16 and read the key verse to the children: "**Where you go, I will go.**" **When Naomi moved to a new place, Ruth went with her.** Look again at Poster H and remind learners to be faithful friends to all of the people they love. Fold hands, close eyes, and thank God for the family of each member of the class by name.

Samuel Listens to God

Session at a Glance	What You Need	What Learners Do
Ready for the Story (15 minutes)		
Welcome the Witnesses	• Sleeping bag or blankets, pillows, storybook, stuffed animals	• Pretend to go to sleep.
Take a Look	• Witness CD (TCK), CD player	• Listen to and identify sounds.
Try This	• Open space, pillows, blankets or sleeping bag	• Play a game of sleeping and waking up.
Explore the Story (15 minutes)		
Story Set-Up	• Leaflet 10 (LR), 2" x 4" (5 cm x 10 cm) fabric pieces, glue sticks	• Make a bed for Samuel.
Storytelling	• Reproducible Sheet C or D (TCK), two craft sticks, markers, scissors, Bible, Leaflet 10 (LR), Witness CD (TCK), CD player, Activity Card B (TCK)	• Hear the story of Eli and Samuel.
I Can Too: Faith Traits	• "Little Book of Faith Traits" booklets (from Session 1), Sticker Sheet 1 (LR)	• Tell a message to someone else and add to their booklets.
Live the Story (30 minutes)		
Ways to Witness	• Leaflet 10 (LR), Sticker Sheet 2 (LR)	• Identify some ways God speaks to them.
Kids Create	• Fabric, round-headed clothespins, fine-tip markers, chenille craft stems, scissors • Poster K (TCK), cardboard, aluminum foil, glue, crayons	• Make a Samuel puppet. • Make a "God Calls Me" mirror.
Worship Together	• Bible, Poster K (TCK), Leaflet 10 (LR)	• Thank God for calling us.

10

Bible Text

1 Samuel 3:1-18

Key Verse

Speak, for your servant is listening.
1 Samuel 3:10b

BIG Idea

God calls us to be truthful.

LR = Learner Resource
TCK = Teacher Class Kit
M&P = Materials and Preparation

Teacher Prayer

Lord, you called Samuel by name. Even as a little boy his heart was open to your call. Help me to listen for your will for my life. Give me the courage to respond as Samuel did. Guide me as I help the children in my class listen to your word. Amen

Question for Reflection

Why would the Lord call a small child to lead the people? Perhaps it is easier for a child to speak the truth. Consider times that you have been brave enough to say what is true.

Learner Goals

KNOW
the story of God calling Samuel

GROW
in their ability to listen to God

SHOW
their love for God in worship and prayer

FACTOID

The Ark of the Covenant in the temple was the symbol of God's presence on earth. The Ark, in some accounts, contained the tablets of the Ten Commandments.

Bible Background

What Factors Shaped This Story?

The child Samuel was an answer to the prayers of Hannah, who had been unable to bear children. Hannah promised that if God gave her a son she would set him apart for service to God. When Samuel was weaned, Hannah took him to Eli, the priest at Shiloh, who became Samuel's guardian and teacher. Eli's own sons stole from those who came to worship at Shiloh. Eli's sons would not inherit a priestly role. Rather, God would raise up another to be a faithful priest in Samuel.

What Is This Story About?

Three times in the night the Lord called Samuel and Samuel mistook the voice of God for that of Eli, his guardian and teacher. Eli discerned that it was God who called Samuel. Eli turned Samuel's attention to God's calling of him and instructed him how to respond. The fourth time God called, Samuel responded as he had been told: "Speak, for your servant is listening" (3:10). God told Samuel of God's plan against Eli's sons for their sins against God. Samuel lay awake with this knowledge till morning, afraid to tell Eli. But the Lord had warned Eli that this would come (2:27-36). When Samuel told Eli everything, Eli responded, "It is the Lord" (3:18), and he knew that the Lord would do what was said.

Why Is This Story Important?

God's call is not always easy to discern. We hear and recognize it with the help of others who recognize that God has a purpose for us, help us listen, and teach us to respond. God has a purpose for each of us. Once we respond, God's call is not always easy to follow. We may be called to tasks we never imagined. We may be called to proclaim an unpopular message. We may be called to reform and transform the teachings and institutions that were the basis of our own education in the faith. We can follow, trusting that when God calls God also makes provision for us.

Age-Level Connection

Two- and three-year-olds may not be surprised that God would talk to a little boy. They may not see themselves as less important than adults. Help them discover that God speaks to us through the Bible, through worship, and through learning experiences. Many people help us find out what God wants us to do.

Ready for the Story (15 minutes)

Welcome the Witnesses

M&P *Prepare an area for pretending to sleep with pillows, blankets or a sleeping bag, stuffed animals, and a storybook.*
Greet the children warmly. Take time to ask about news that the learners have to share. Direct their attention to the area you have set up for sleeping. Suggest that the children pretend to go to bed. Sit nearby and talk with the children about bedtime. Point to the storybook and the stuffed animals. **What do you do with these things at bedtime? Where do you sleep? Does anyone take a teddy bear or other friend to bed? The Bible story today tells about a little boy named Samuel. The story tells us what happened when Samuel went to bed one night.**

Take a Look

M&P *Set up a CD player and have the Witness CD from the Age 2–Grade 4 Teacher Class Kit (TCK) ready to play.*
Gather together in the storytelling area. **Use your ears to listen. Listen to the sounds and see if you can guess what is making each sound.** Play Track 17, "Creature Sounds," on the CD. Pause after each sound and give the children time to name what they hear. Listen for any sounds coming from the area around the classroom.

Try This

M&P *Have the pillows and blankets from Welcome the Witnesses on the floor.*
Suggest that everyone lie down on the blankets or sleeping bag. Turn out the lights and pretend to go to sleep. Call one child's name by saying: _______, **wake up!** Continue until you have called everyone's name. If the children enjoy this game, play again.

With everyone "awake," sing more stanzas of "Spread the Good News," introduced on page 9. Sing, "God calls me," from page 43, and see other stanzas on pages 10, 15, and 20 also.

Witness WORDS

Samuel, temple, listening

FACTOID

Lord represents four Hebrew letters *hwhy*, transliterated YHWH and pronounced Yahweh (yaw-way), which is the name God told to Moses in Exodus 3:14.

Transition Tip

Ask each child to call one other child to the table, saying that child's name three times, to get ready for the story.

Explore the Story (15 minutes)

Story Set-Up

M&P *Have a Leaflet 10 from the Ages 2-3 Learner Resource (LR) and a 2" x 4" (5 cm x 10 cm) piece of fabric ready for each child, along with glue sticks.*
When Samuel was a little boy, his mother took him to live at the temple, a building something like our church. Samuel lived with a man named Eli. Samuel and Eli worked and played at the temple. They ate at the temple and went to sleep there at night. Have the learners find the picture of Samuel sleeping on the front of the leaflet and glue the top long edge of the fabric over Samuel's blanket to keep him warm.

Storytelling

M&P *Copy two figures on Reproducible Sheet C or D (TCK)—one to be Samuel and one to be Eli—then color them, cut them out, and attach each to a craft stick. Have a Bible and Leaflet 10 on hand as well as a CD player, the Witness CD, and the pieces from Activity Card B (TCK).*
Call the children together in the storytelling area. Open the Bible to 1 Samuel 3. **This Bible story tells us what happened when Samuel went to bed one night.** Introduce the figures of Samuel and Eli, and remind learners that Eli was the person at the temple who took care of Samuel. Use the figures to illustrate the action of the story inside the leaflet as you tell it. Encourage the children to help you call Samuel each time. Allow time for the children to talk about the story or share their experiences. You may want to play the "Wake Up Call" narration, Track 10, on the CD as you review the story using the puzzle pieces from Activity Card B.

I Can Too: FAITH Traits

M&P *Have out the "Little Book of Faith Traits" (see page 9) and the Session 10 sticker from Sticker Sheet 1 (LR) for each child*
God called Samuel to give him an important message. The message told Samuel what God wanted the people to do. Let's play a game with messages. I will give each of you a message and then you can tell the message to everyone. Call one child to your side. Whisper a message into the child's ear such as "God loves you." Have the child share the message with the others. Vary the messages to include things such as "God cares for you" or "God hears you when you pray."

Today's Faith Trait is honesty. Samuel was honest and told Eli God's message. You all were honest and shared your messages too. Distribute the booklets and give each child a Session 10 sticker. Comment on the activity idea and help them add the stickers to page 10. Collect the booklets for use later.

Kid Connect

Samuel told Eli what God said. Telling the truth comes easily for young children since they have neither the understanding nor the skill to change the truth. Be sure to thank children for telling what really happened even when the truth may not be pleasant. Examples might include being able to admit to taking a toy or hurting another child.

More Movement

Have everyone stand up. Have one adult stand on the other side of the room. One by one call the children to you. Give each of them the message "God loves you." Encourage the children to run to the other adult and share the message, just as Samuel did.

Live the Story (30 minutes)

Ways to Witness

M&P *Have a Leaflet 10 and the ears stickers from Sticker Sheet 2 (LR) for each child.*

Provide the learners with copies of the leaflet and help them find the illustrations of children inside. **Look at these pictures of ways that God talks to us.** Talk with the children about what is happening in each illustration. Help the learners add ear stickers by the pictures that show ways they listen to God.

Kids Create

M&P *Samuel Puppet: You will need a round-headed clothespin, a chenille craft stem, a 4" x 6" (10 cm x 15 cm) and a 2" x 6" (5 cm x 15 cm) piece of fabric for each learner. Cut a 1" (2.5 cm) slit across the center of the smaller fabric for the clothespin head. Have fine-tip markers out.*

"God Calls Me" Mirror: Display Poster K (TCK). Cut a 6" x 10" (15 cm x 25 cm) cardboard hand-mirror shape for each child (see Poster K). Also cut a 5"(13 cm) circle of aluminum foil for each child. Have glue and crayons available.

Samuel Puppet: Give each learner a round-headed clothespin. **Who could we pretend this person is?** *(Accept all responses but work toward the idea that this could be Samuel.)* Show the children how to slip the smaller piece of fabric over the clothespin. Help them wrap a chenille craft stem securely around the clothespin to form arms, and add features with markers, if they wish. Offer them each a second piece of fabric for Samuel's blanket. **Let's put our Samuels to bed.** Then call, "Samuel!" three times.

"God Calls Me" Mirror: Direct everyone's attention to Poster K and name those who are called. **God does call you because God loves and cares for you. Will you remember to listen? Let's make "God Calls Me" mirrors to help remember.** Hand out the cardboard mirror shapes and help learners glue on the foil circles. As they add crayon decorations, print "God Calls ———" with her or his name on the handle of each child's mirror. **Keep your mirrors where you can see them and remember to listen for God's word.**

Worship Together

M&P *Display Poster K and have a Bible and one Leaflet 10 handy.*

Sit together in the storytelling area. Open the Bible to 1 Samuel and show the children where the name *Samuel* is printed on the page. **The Bible tells us what Samuel said to God. Do you remember? He said, "Speak, for your servant is listening."** Point to Poster K and read the words. **God called Samuel; God also called Gideon. Who else does God call? You.** Then fold hands and pray together the prayer on the back of the leaflet.

Teacher Boost

Listening isn't always easy for young learners. You are helping them hear and see, hear and touch, and hear and do. Whenever you make use of several of the children's senses, you increase the likelihood that they will learn more than if you just talked to them.

Witnesses in the World

Find pictures or photographs of people worshiping in various places or environments. Talk with the learners about what the people in the pictures are doing. Remind the children that everyone comes to worship to listen to God and to talk to God.

GREAT good byes

Gather the items that the children will take home. At the door, bend down and whisper a special message to each child: **I'll see you next week.** Offer hugs or handshakes as children leave with family members.

David and Goliath

11

Bible Text

1 Samuel 17:4-11, 32-50

Key Verse

I come to you in the name of the Lord. 1 Samuel 17:45b

BIG Idea

God wants us to stand up for others.

LR = Learner Resource
TCK = Teacher Class Kit
M&P = Materials and Preparation

Session at a Glance	What You Need	What Learners Do
Ready for the Story (15 minutes)		
Welcome the Witnesses	• Large sheet of paper, tape, markers, stickers, yardstick or meterstick	• Measure how big they are.
Take a Look	• Large sheet of paper, crayons or markers	• Make a paper giant.
Try This	• Large open space	• Play a game taking large and small steps.
Explore the Story (15 minutes)		
Story Set-Up	• Leaflet 11 (LR), craft sticks, glue	• Make David, the shep-herd.
Storytelling	• Poster I (TCK), Activity Card C (TCK), scissors, Leaflet 11 (LR), paper giant, Witness CD (TCK), CD player	• Hear the story of David and the giant.
I Can Too: Faith Traits	• Large open space, "Little Book of Faith Traits" booklets (from Session 1), Sticker Sheet 1 (LR)	• Play a game about David and the giant and add to their booklets.
Live the Story (30 minutes)		
Ways to Witness	• Leaflet 11 (LR), Sticker Sheet 2 (LR)	• Identify some times that they are brave.
Kids Create	• Five small stones and a margarine lid for each child, sand, glue, craft sticks • Black construction paper, scissors, coffee filters, washable markers, spray bottle of water, glue	• Make five small stones. • Make silhouettes.
Worship Together	• Bible, masks from Activity Card C (TCK)	• Thank God for keeping them safe.

Bible Background

What Factors Shaped This Story?

Under Samuel's leadership the ancient Israelites demanded from God a king like the other nations. The first king was Saul whom Samuel anointed, but Saul proved unworthy. The Lord sent Samuel to the house of Jesse in Bethlehem, where Samuel would find the new king. That king was David, a shepherd and Jesse's youngest son. The story of David and Goliath is that of David's first military victory.

What Is This Story About?

Imagine the biggest, most heavily armed, most powerful and frightening warrior you can. That was Goliath the Philistine. He was almost 10 feet (3 meters) tall. Goliath challenged the Israelites to send someone to do battle with him. Whoever won the fight would make servants of the opponent's people. The Israelites quaked with fear.

David was young and not the most experienced, but he volunteered. He figured that if he could protect the sheep from lions and bears, he could handle Goliath. David trusted that God would protect him as God had done in the past. Unaccustomed to military armor and weaponry, David went in his shepherd's garb and with his shepherd's staff and bag, in which he placed five stones for use in his slingshot—hardly an adequate weapon against Goliath. Goliath came to do battle with David, who drew out his slingshot, hit Goliath square in the forehead, and won the battle.

Why Is This Story Important?

What is the source of real power? We tend to think that military might, wealth, and political power rule the world. None of these amounts to anything beside the power of God on which David relied. This story is not so much about God taking up arms against human beings as it is about the real nature of power. God stands with those who appear to be weak and brings to naught those who wield the power of this world.

Age-Level Connection

The story of David and Goliath is amazing in its outcome. However, young children face all kinds of giants in everyday life. Keep in mind that the learners may have real fears about people and things that could hurt them. Remind the children that God took care of David and God promises to take care of us too.

Teacher Prayer

Dear God, I am amazed at the courage young David showed. His trust in you led David to do something that seemed impossible to everyone around him. Give me courage to do the things that seem too difficult for me to do. Amen

Question for Reflection

What tasks seem impossible in your life? Imagine how God might help you find the courage to tackle a problem or situation that troubles you.

Learner Goals

KNOW
about the brave boy, David

GROW
in their belief that God cares for them

SHOW
love for another member of the class

FACTOID

A cubit, about 17½" (44 centimeters), equals two spans. A span is three handbreadths. A handbreadth is four fingers. Some say a cubit equals seven (rather than six) handbreadths.

Ready for the Story (15 minutes)

Witness WORDS

David, giant, Lord

FACTOID

Greaves are armor for one's shins.

Welcome the Witnesses

M&P *Attach a 6' (1.8 m) strip of paper to a wall or door where you are able to measure children. Have a yardstick or meterstick, markers, and stickers available.*

Greet the children by name and welcome them into the classroom. Show them the yardstick or meterstick. **Does anyone know what this is? Can you show how to use it?** Invite each learner to stand next to the sheet of paper and mark how tall he or she is. Comment on how each one is growing. Print the learners' names next to their marks. Give each child a sticker to help identify his or her height. Remember to measure the adults in the group too.

Take a Look

M&P *On a large sheet of paper draw an outline of a person about 9' (2.7 m) tall. Spread the paper with the drawing on the floor in your class area. Have crayons or markers available.*

Direct the children to the outline of the person. Notice how big this person is. Ask for volunteers to lie down next to the outline. **How do you feel next to someone so big? The Bible story today tells about a boy named David. One day David met a very, very big man named Goliath. David was much smaller but he was not afraid of Goliath.** Distribute crayons or markers and color the giant. Have an adult add scary facial features to the drawing.

Try This

M&P *Make arrangements to play in a large, open space.*

Move to an open space. **When we walk we can take big steps or little steps, giant steps or baby steps.** Demonstrate baby steps and giant steps and have the children try them. Then gather the children on one side of the room with you opposite them. **Take one baby step toward me. Now take one giant step.** Continue alternating steps until all the children have crossed the room. Play again if the children enjoy the game.

Review the "Spread the Good News" song, introduced on page 9 with stanzas added on pages 10, 15, 20, and 43. Sing a "God makes me strong" stanza here.

Transition Tip

Have all the children help move the paper giant to the storytelling area. Use loops of masking tape to attach the giant to the wall. Request that helpers distribute leaflets, craft sticks, and glue sticks.

Explore the Story (15 minutes)

Story Set-Up

M&P *Have available a copy of Leaflet 11 from the Ages 2-3 Learner Resource (LR) for each learner, craft sticks, and glue.*
Hand out Leaflet 11 and look together at the front. **Does anyone know what this boy's name is?** *(David.)* **David has an important job in his family. Look at the picture and see what animals David cares for.** *(Sheep, lambs.)* **David is a shepherd. Let's give him a staff to help him show the sheep where to go.** Provide craft sticks for the children to glue in David's hand.

Storytelling

M&P *Display Poster I from the Age 2–Grade 4 Teacher Class Kit (TCK). Cut out the double-sided mask from Activity Card C (TCK) and cut open the eye holes. Have one Leaflet 11 and the paper giant you made earlier with you for the storytelling. Have a CD player and the Witness CD (TCK) ready if you plan to play the story narration.*
Gather in the storytelling area and look at Poster I. **David, the shepherd boy, cared for his family's sheep. He helped the sheep find food and water, and kept them safe. Do you see any sheep on the poster?** *(No.)* **Today's Bible story is about a time when David helped keep his family and many other people safe.** Read the story inside the leaflet. Refer to the giant the children made earlier when you talk about Goliath, and hold the appropriate mask in front of your face when David and Goliath speak. Include time for comments and questions from the learners. You may also want to play Track 11 on the Witness CD, the story narration "Todd's Tall Tale."

I Can Too: FAITH|Traits

M&P *You will need the "Little Book of Faith Traits" booklets (see page 9) and the Session 11 sticker from Sticker Sheet 1 (LR) for each child.*
Encourage the children to think about how David felt. **Let's pretend to be David and play with some sheep. How do you think David felt?** *(Happy.)* **Now let's pretend that we see the giant. Look at how big the giant is. How do you think David felt when he saw the giant?** *(Afraid, scared.)* **Let's pretend that we go to see our family. Everyone is afraid and hiding in the house. How do you think David felt?** *(Sad.)* **Let's pretend to be David. Let's walk up to the giant. Let's shout, "I come in the name of the Lord." How do you think David felt then?** *(Brave, strong.)*

The Faith Trait for today is responsibility. David took responsibility for caring for God's people the way he had been taking care of his family's sheep. Hand out the booklets and help each children attach the Session 11 sticker to page 11. Talk about the activity suggested and then collect the booklets for use in other sessions.

Kid Connect

It isn't easy for two- and three-year-olds to be brave. Many of their experiences are new and unexpected. From season to season, they may forget what thunder, lightning, and snow are like. Children develop courage when they believe that family members and other adults will keep them safe and protect them.

More Movement

Pretend to be sheep. Invite one learner to be David and care for the sheep, directing the sheep to water to drink and grass to eat. Give everyone who wishes to participate a turn to be David.

Teacher Boost

The stories of the Old Testament introduce many people, old and young, who believed in God. The time you spend with the children helps them grow in their understanding that God calls all of us to be children of God. You are helping them identify ways they can show and share their love for God.

Witnesses in the World

Attach a piece of poster board to a wall or bulletin board, and on it print the words, "Dear God, please take care of. . . ." During the week check the newspaper for photographs of people who are ill, hungry, homeless, or living in underdeveloped parts of the world. Invite the learners to add the pictures to the poster. Include these individuals in your group prayers.

GREAT good byes

Invite family members to come see the giant. Say good-bye to each of the learners and offer a hug or a handshake. **Remember, God will be with you during the coming week.**

Live the Story (30 minutes)

Ways to Witness

M&P *Have a leaflet and the medal stickers from Sticker Sheet 2 (LR) for each child.*

David was a brave, young boy. The Bible tells us that David trusted God to take care of him and protect him. Look inside the leaflet at the illustrations. **When are you brave?** Talk about situations such as during a storm, going to the doctor, or approaching a large dog. **What helps you feel brave?** Help children add the medal stickers next to the pictures of times they try to be brave.

Kids Create

M&P *Five Small Stones: Gather a plastic margarine lid and five small stones for each child. You will also need glue, craft sticks, and some clean sand.*

Silhouettes: Cut a 3" (7.5 cm) tall and a 5" (13 cm) tall person figure from black construction paper for each child. You will also need a coffee filter for each child, washable markers, a spray bottle of water, and glue.

Five Small Stones: What did David use to defeat Goliath? *(A sling and stones.)* Provide a small plastic margarine lid for each child. Have the learners spread some glue on their lids with craft sticks. Sprinkle sand on top of the glue. Have each child count out five small stones, add more glue, if needed, and attach the stones to the lid. **These stones can help you remember that God cares for you just as God cared for David.**

Silhouettes: Give each child a paper coffee filter and set out washable markers. **Use these markers to color the center of your filter.** Gently spray completed drawings with a fine mist. **What happened to your colors?** Guide the children to see how the water made the colors blend to make a design. Have available the small and large person figures cut from black construction paper. **Who do these figures make you think of?** *(David and Goliath.)* When the filter has dried, show the children how to glue the figures to the center. **Let's practice using your silhouettes to tell the story of David and the giant. Then you can do it at home.**

Worship Together

M&P *Have a Bible and the double-sided mask from Activity Card C available.*

Give learners jobs to help straighten the room and then gather in the storytelling area. **God helped David feel brave. Can you think of a time that you were brave?** *(Affirm all responses.)* Open the Bible to 1 Samuel and read the key verse: **I come to you in the name of the Lord.** Let each child hold up the David mask and say the verse. **These words David said told Goliath that David was not alone. God was with David. God is always with us too.** Fold hands and pray together for each member of the class: **Thank you, God, for being with ________.** *(Name each person.)* **Amen**

Daniel and the Lions

12

Session at a Glance	What You Need	What Learners Do
Ready for the Story (15 minutes)		
Welcome the Witness	• Books with pictures of animals, stuffed animals, cardboard boxes	• Examine different kinds of animals.
Take a Look	• Scented and unscented candles, matches	• Investigate smells.
Try This	• Open space	• Play Follow the Leader.
Explore the Story (15 minutes)		
Story Set-Up	• Leaflet 12 (LR), crayon or marker	• Trace their hands.
Storytelling	• Bible, Leaflet 12 (LR), Witness CD (TCK), CD player, Poster J (TCK)	• Help tell the story of Daniel.
I Can Too: Faith Traits	• "Little Book of Faith Traits" booklets (from Session 1), Sticker Sheet 1 (LR)	• Sing "Spread the Good News" and add to their booklets.
Live the Story (30 minutes)		
Ways to Witness	• Leaflet 12 (LR), Sticker Sheet 2 (LR), Poster N (TCK)	• Learn about God's care and find things to pray about.
Kids Create	• Letter-size construction paper, stickers, markers or crayons • Small paper plates, crayons, short pieces of yellow or brown yarn, glue sticks	• Make prayer cards. • Make lion masks.
Worship Together	• Bible, Leaflet 12 (LR)	• Thank God for keeping us safe.

Bible Text

Daniel 6

Key Verse

My God sent his angel and shut the lions' mouths so that they would not hurt me. Daniel 6:22a

BIG Idea

God keeps us safe.

LR = Learner Resource
TCK = Teacher Class Kit
M&P = Materials and Preparation

Teacher Prayer

Dear God, there haven't been many times that I have been afraid to say that I believe in you. Yet, I know that there are times when I have not stood up or spoken up when I should. Help me to develop a strong faith that gives me courage to show my love for you. Amen

Question for Reflection

Are you able to identify a time when you were afraid of what others might think about your belief in God? Recall what you did in that situation.

Learner Goals

KNOW
about brave Daniel and the lions

GROW
in their understanding that God hears prayer

SHOW
that they are learning to pray to God

FACTOID

Darius planned to appoint Daniel over the satraps, who governed the empire's provinces. Each had a military and a civil leader serving under the satrap.

Bible Background

What Factors Shaped This Story?

The book of Daniel was written to encourage the people of God when they were oppressed and exploited. The first six chapters tell six stories of the faithful young Daniel. He and others faced repeated persecutions. Each time God rescued them. These stories referred to the people's past in exile. Chapters 7–12 tell four stories to address more contemporary persecutions that the people suffered under the Greek imperial occupation of their land. Antiochus IV Epiphanes was a brutal ruler intent on turning Jerusalem from a holy place for the people of God into a monument to the Greek gods. The stories again teach that God is sovereign and will protect and deliver the people.

What Is This Story About?

Daniel was the most excellent among King Darius's administrators. Darius planned to give him the highest position, and the other administrators became jealous. Daniel was also a pious person and faithful to God. The other administrators tried to use Daniel's faithfulness against him. They came to Darius proposing a new ordinance that no one should pray—except to Darius—for 30 days. They said that all his administrators were in favor. They were lying, of course, since Daniel knew nothing of this. No doubt flattered, Darius signed the ordinance. Daniel didn't comply because of his faithfulness to God. The conspirators wanted Daniel thrown to the lions. Darius was powerless to rescue Daniel, even though Darius himself put the ordinance into effect. That didn't matter because God was faithful to Daniel and protected him in the lions' den. Daniel's enemies were thrown into the lions' den, and Darius became a worshiper of Daniel's God.

Why Is This Story Important?

Daniel's faithfulness was used against him. God was faithful to Daniel and protected him. Acting on his faith was Daniel's witness to Darius, who saw the power of God to save. The power of kings is finally subject to the power of God.

Age-Level Connection

The children are beginning to understand that they can talk to God in prayer. Many of their prayers are words of thanks. Guide the children to see that there are many times that they can pray, such as when they are afraid or when they need help.

Ready for the Story (15 minutes)

Welcome the Witnesses

M&P *Bring a variety of stuffed animals and books about animals. Locate several cardboard boxes to serve as homes for the stuffed animals.*
Greet the children cheerfully with a stuffed animal. Have the animal say hello too. Give each child a turn to hold the animal. Direct their attention to the books that you brought in. Sit down on the floor with the children and look at the pictures in the books. **What animals can you name? Do any animals live in your homes? What animals have you seen in other places?** Encourage play with the animals and the boxes.

Take a Look

M&P *Gather some scented candles and matches. Check with caregivers for any learners who have fragrance sensitivities, and provide unscented candles as necessary. Before lighting candles, check your local fire codes and your congregation's fire policies regarding the use of open flame.*
Show the children the candles you gathered. Give everyone a turn to smell the different smells. **Which ones do you like? Sometimes, people light candles when they pray. The smell and the light of the candles help people think about God.** Light one candle for the children to see, if appropriate. **When we see a candle, the candle helps us remember that God is with us. God listens when we pray.**

Try This

Invite everyone to play the game Follow the Leader. **Watch the leader and do what the leader does.** Try a variety of actions, making sure all of them are doable for everyone in the group. As you come to the end of the game, fold hands. **What do we do when we fold our hands?** *(We pray.)* **Who do we talk to when we pray?** *(God.)* **Today's Bible story is about a man named Daniel who prayed to God often.**

Witness WORDS

Daniel, prayer, lions' den

FACTOID

Daniel's three daily prayers would have been morning, midday, and evening. Christian tradition includes up to nine prayer times throughout the day and night.

Transition Tip

Select two of the learners to help distribute leaflets. Another child might set out crayons or markers.

Explore the Story (15 minutes)

Kid Connect

Two- and three-year-olds are concrete thinkers. It may be difficult for them to believe that God, who they cannot see, can hear their prayers. Here is an opportunity to help the children grasp that there are things that even adults are not able to understand. We pray to God because the Bible tells us that God hears our prayers.

More Movement

Pretend to be lions. Try crawling, leaping, and growling like lions. Imagine what Daniel might have seen and heard in the lions' den.

Story Set-Up

M&P *Have Leaflet 12 from each Ages 2-3 Learner Resource (LR) and a crayon or marker available.*
Hand out the leaflets and look at the front page. **What do you do with your hands when you pray? Some people fold their hands and others place their palms together. Holding our hands a certain way when we pray can help us think about God. Our hands can help us remember to listen to God and talk to God.** Have the children place their hands in the frame on the front of their leaflets while you trace around them with a crayon or marker. **Show us how you like to fold your hands.**

Storytelling

M&P *Have a Bible and a copy of Leaflet 12 available. Set up the CD player with the Witness CD from the Age 2–Grade 4 Teacher Class Kit (TCK) ready to play. Display Poster J (TCK) in the storytelling area.*
Move to the storytelling area and point to Poster J. **What does this poster remind you of?** *(A movie poster.)* **Does this look like a happy movie or a scary one?** *(Probably scary.)* Open the Bible to the book of Daniel. Show the children the word *Daniel.* **Part of the Bible is called the book of Daniel. The book of Daniel tells us about a very brave man whose name was Daniel.** Read the story inside the leaflet. Allow time for the comments and questions the learners may wish to share. Play the story song on the Witness CD, "Here Kitty, Kitty" (Track 12). Learners will enjoy singing the refrain.

I Can Too: FAITH Traits

M&P *You will need the "Little Book of Faith Traits" booklets (see page 9) and the Session 12 sticker from Sticker Sheet 1 (LR) for each child.*
Sing the song "Spread the Good News" from page 9 with the stanzas already introduced (see page 58). Then sing a new stanza: "God hears me pray, God hears me pray, spread the good news, God hears me pray." **The Bible tells us that God promises to hear us when we pray. That is great news to share.**

The Faith Trait for today is honesty. Daniel was honest about his love for God, even when it got him in trouble. He told the truth about praying to God every day. Do you tell the truth? Distribute the booklets and Session 12 stickers. Help learners attach the stickers to page 12 as you comment on the activity suggestion. Collect the booklets for use in later sessions.

Live the Story (30 minutes)

Ways to Witness

M&P *Display Poster N (TCK). Have the leaflets and the hands stickers from each Sticker Sheet 2 (LR) available.*

Gather near Poster N and invite conversation about the things that keep people safe. Offer whatever explanations the learners need to understand the items pictured on the poster and how they are used. **God sends people and things to help care for you and keep you safe every day.**

Distribute the leaflets and the hands stickers. **The Bible story tells us that God kept Daniel safe.** Look at the pictures inside the leaflet. **What do these pictures show?** *(Daytime, nighttime, mealtime, and sick time.)* Help the children identify times they can pray and add a sticker by each.

Kids Create

M&P *Prayer Cards: Have out sheets of letter-size construction paper, stickers, and crayons or markers.*

Lion Masks: Have small paper plates, crayons, short pieces of yellow or brown yarn, and glue sticks available.

Prayer Cards: Distribute construction paper and help each child fold the paper in half the long way. Show how the card can stand up like a tent. On each side of the tents, horizontally print the words, "Thank you, God, for...." **Tell me what things you want to thank God for and I'll print them on your cards. Then you can use stickers and crayons or markers for decorating. Set your prayer cards where they can remind you to thank God at home.**

Lion Masks: Let's make lion masks. Give each child a paper plate. Provide crayons for coloring. Offer glue sticks for attaching short pieces of yellow or brown yarn to make the mane around the lion's face. **Hold the mask up to your face and pretend to be a lion.** Have a volunteer pretend to be Daniel, surrounded by growling "lions." Another child can be an angel who taps each lion to close its mouth.

Worship Together

M&P *Have a Bible and a leaflet on hand.*

When the room is straightened, open the Bible to the book of Daniel and read the key verse for this session: **My God sent his angel and shut the lions' mouths so that they would not hurt me.** Then ask: **How do you think Daniel felt when he was with the lions? Do you think he was afraid?** *(Accept all responses.)* **What did Daniel do when he was afraid?** *(He prayed.)* **We can pray to God when we are afraid too.** Close with the prayer on the back of the leaflet.

Teacher Boost

This may be a good time to share some of the ups and downs of your faith with your learners. Emphasize that God always has faith in us!

Witnesses in the World

Locate a map of the world. Display the map at the children's eye level. Explain that we can pray for people who live near us and far away. Point to the place where you live and name that place for the children. Give each learner an opportunity to point to another place on the map. Name each location and remind the children that we can pray for the people who live there.

Go Global!

Read the Go Global! activity on Reproducible Sheets S and T (TCK). See page 3.

GREAT goodbyes

Gather the items that the children have made. Greet family members and ask them to bring photos of their children for use in a later session. Say to each child: **Good-bye, ________. I will pray for you this week.** Offer a hug or a handshake.

The Peaceful Kingdom

13

Bible Text
Isaiah 11:1-9

Key Verse
The wolf shall live with the lamb.
Isaiah 11:6a

BIG Idea

God promises us peace.

LR = Learner Resource
TCK = Teacher Class Kit
M&P = Materials and Preparation

Session at a Glance	What You Need	What Learners Do
Explore the Story (15 minutes)		
Welcome the Witnesses	• Containers, sand, plastic table covering, small animal figures, CD player, Witness CD (TCK)	• Play with toy animals.
Take a Look	• Tree branch, large flowerpot, stones or sand, green paper, masking tape	• Make a classroom tree.
Try This	• Open space, Poster M (TCK)	• Pretend to be animals.
Explore the Story (15 minutes)		
Story Set-Up	• Leaflet 13 (LR), Sticker Sheet 2 (LR), fabric, items of different textures like animal skins, glue sticks	• Wonder about animal skins.
Storytelling	• Poster A (TCK), Leaflet 13 (LR), Bible, CD player, Witness CD (TCK)	• Hear the story of the peaceful kingdom.
I Can Too: Faith Traits	• CD of peaceful music, CD player, "Little Book of Faith Traits" booklets (from Session 1), Sticker Sheet 1 (LR)	• Relax in peaceful ways and add to their booklets.
Live the Story (30 minutes)		
Ways to Witness	• A time to visit with the pastor	• Learn about sharing the peace.
Kids Create	• Cardboard, pencil, glue, light blue construction paper, dark blue crayons • Mural paper or poster board, pictures of animals, glue sticks, markers	• Make doves of peace. • Make a Peaceful Kingdom collage.
Worship Together	• Bible, Leaflet 13 (LR), Kids Create project	• Make a peace circle for prayer.

Bible Background

What Factors Shaped This Story?

The prophet Isaiah spoke during the latter eighth and early ninth centuries B.C.E. During Isaiah's time the Israelites lived under the power and threat of the Assyrian empire. There was also failure of faith and attendant injustice among the people. Isaiah foretells both of the reality of external threat and of internal threat in the people's life. Isaiah prophesies God's punishment against the people's arrogance and injustice and foretells God's deliverance of the people from their enemies. God's will is for a faithful people living in justice and peace.

What Is This Story About?

Though God seems absent when the people are rebellious and when they suffer oppression, Isaiah says that a new time will come. God will deliver them from their oppression. Their enemies will be destroyed. A child will be born the Messiah king, who will bring justice, righteousness, and peace. The Messiah will be a descendant of David and of Jesse, David's father. The spirit of the Lord will be present with this leader. The leader will have the gifts of wisdom, understanding, counsel, might, knowledge, and fear of the Lord. The leader will bring justice for the poor and meek; the wicked will be destroyed. Creation will be made new. Peace will come and be realized in all creation. Those who now seem to be "natural" enemies will live together, even sleep alongside one another in safety. They will eat together and raise their young together. All creation will know God. The knowledge of God will be as much a part of creation as water is part of the sea.

Why Is This Story Important?

There is hope. Isaiah prophesied that God protects and provides for the people against both their external enemies and their own faithlessness and rebellion. God never abandoned the ancient Israelites and will not abandon us. God brings judgment, justice, and restoration. God raises up leaders who see God's vision of wholeness.

Age-Level Connection

Peace is a sophisticated concept for two- and three-year-olds. Encourage acts of kindness and caring in your classroom when the learners will feel loved and cared for. Point out examples of sharing and caring so that the children begin to recognize the behaviors that make for peace.

Teacher Prayer

Lord, we live in a world that talks about peace, but sometimes peace is hard to find. Help me to see ways that I can live in peace with my family, my neighbors, and the world. Let shoots of peace take root in my heart and in the hearts of the learners. Amen

Question for Reflection

Think of an uncomfortable situation in your home, work, or neighborhood. What is one thing you might do to bring harmony where it is needed?

Learner Goals

KNOW
that God wants us to have peace

GROW
in their knowledge that God wants us to love others

SHOW
one way of sharing the peace

FACTOID

God promised that Israel's king would always come from the family of King David.

Ready for the Story (15 minutes)

Witness WORDS

peace, promise

Welcome the Witnesses

M&P *Partially fill several containers with sand. Find a variety of small toy animals and place them in the sandboxes. Protect a low table or an area of the floor with a plastic covering, and set the sandboxes on it. Locate a CD player and the Witness CD from the Age 2–Grade 4 Teacher Class Kit (TCK).* Greet the learners with animal sounds such as gentle mewing, baaing, or barking. **What kind of animal do you think I am? Look in these sandboxes and play with the animals you see. Talk with each other about the different animals. Do your animals get along? You all seem to be getting along.** Play Track 17, "Creature Sounds," on the Witness CD while they play. Look for examples of sharing and taking turns. Thank the children for showing kindness toward others.

FACTOID
The Bible does not mention the death of Isaiah, nor of any other of the prophets, maybe to show that their books are of undying relevance.

Take a Look

M&P *Find a tree limb with several branches. Secure the limb in a large flowerpot with stones or sand. Have green construction paper and masking tape on hand.*

The Bible story today tells us about a young tree that is growing. Let's try making a tree like the one in the Bible story. Show the children how to tear pieces of green construction paper into leaf shapes. Provide pieces of tape children can use to attach the leaves to the branches. Involve everyone in making the tree. Admire the children's efforts.

Try This

M&P *Make arrangements to use an open space. Locate Poster M (TCK).* Move to an open space. **The Bible story today tells us about animals. Let's pretend that we can be different kinds of animals.** Try moving in different ways such as crawling like bears, hopping like rabbits, waddling like ducks, and slithering like snakes. **Do all animals like each other? What are some animals that other animals are afraid of?** Offer suggestions if younger children can't think of any examples. **What do cats do when a dog comes near them? Where do rabbits go when a fox comes by? What do you think a giraffe would do if it saw a lion?**

Back in your room, look together at Poster M. **This is an imaginary animal. Can you find pieces of it that come from animals we know?** Invite comments. **What would be a good name for this animal?** *(Accept all responses.)*

Transition Tip

Move back to the class area pretending that you are birds flying through the air. Encourage the children to fly smoothly without bumping into one another. Select helpers to distribute leaflets.

Explore the Story (15 minutes)

Story Set-Up

M&P *Have Leaflet 13 from the Ages 2-3 Learner Resource (LR) and the animal-skin sticker from Sticker Sheet 2 (LR) for each child. Collect a supply of fabric swatches and other materials that resemble animal skins, such as cotton, wool, satin, feathers, leather, or sandpaper. Set out glue sticks.*

Hand out the leaflets and look at the front page. **What animals do you see? Feel these textures and think about the animals those textures make you think of.** Help the children attach the appropriate animal-skin sticker and then glue on other materials if they wish. Talk about ways that the animals feel different, move in different ways, and make different sounds. **God planned for the world to have all kinds of animals. People are all different and animals are different too.**

Storytelling

M&P *Display Poster A (TCK) on a bulletin board or wall near the storytelling area. Locate a Bible, Leaflet 13, a CD player, and the Witness CD.*

Gather the learners together in the storytelling area. **Do you remember this poster and these pictures of God's creation? Today's Bible story is more about God's wonderful world.** Invite each child to come to the poster and name one of the animals. Open the Bible to the book of Isaiah and then read the story inside the leaflet. Listen to the comments and questions that the children wish to share. Then play Track 13 on the Witness CD, "The Peaceful Kingdom Comes" story narration.

I Can Too: FAITH Traits

M&P *Locate a CD of peaceful music and set up the CD player. Have the "Little Book of Faith Traits" booklets (see page 9) and the Session 13 sticker from Sticker Sheet 1 (LR) for each child.*

The Bible tells us that some day all the animals will live happily together. Then people will live together in peace too. There will be no fighting or anger or sadness. Play the peaceful music you brought in, and suggest that everyone dance in peaceful ways together. After a couple of minutes, invite the children to sit down. **Now let's close our eyes while we listen to the music again, and imagine animals moving together peacefully.**

The Faith Trait for today is peace. God loves peace and wants all of us to live peacefully. Have you worked and played peacefully with someone today? Affirm any positive behavior you have seen among the learners as you hand out their booklets. Help each one attach the Session 13 sticker to page 13 as you read the activity idea. Collect the booklets to use again in later sessions.

Sing "Spread the Good News," introduced on page 9. Use the "God gives us peace" stanza. Use the stanzas on pages 15 and 64 too.

Kid Connect

Peace comes to young children when they are fed, rested, and playing happily. Two- and three-year-olds are beginning to try showing love for each other. Look for opportunities to give a gentle pat or hug or to share kind words such as "You are my friend," "Please," or "Thank you." Children tend to behave in ways modeled by the adults around them.

More Movement

Play a sharing game. Give a ball or beanbag to one child and have him or her toss it onto a chair or into a basket. Then ask the child to pick it up and share it with a friend. Repeat until everyone in the class has had a turn. Playing peacefully with friends is fun.

Teacher Boost

Remember that you are planting seeds of peace, whether you see the seedlings actually emerge or not.

Witnesses in the World

Learn about projects that your congregation participates in that support children in other parts of the world. Share information with families about school kits, layettes, or vitamin collections that provide items for children elsewhere.

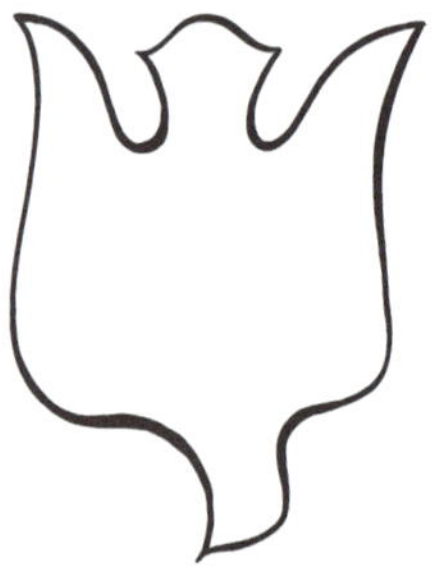

Outline for Doves of Peace

GREAT good byes

Gather up papers and projects. At the door say good-bye with the words, **The peace of the Lord be with you.** Offer each learner a hug or a handshake. Ask family members to provide photos of their children for the next session.

Live the Story (30 minutes)

Ways to Witness

M&P *Make arrangements for a brief visit with the pastor to learn about passing the peace. If possible, meet him or her in the sanctuary.*
Many people help us learn about the peace of the Lord. One of these people is the pastor of our church. Let's go see the pastor and talk about peace. Walk to the sanctuary or wherever you arranged to meet the pastor. Introduce the pastor and encourage the children to tell their names. Ask the pastor to demonstrate how people share the peace of the Lord in worship, and say the words of peace. Practice sharing the peace with each other.

Kids Create

M&P *Doves of Peace: Draw a simple 4" x 4" (10 cm x 10 cm) dove outline on several pieces of cardboard and then trace the outline with a thick, solid line of white glue so the figure is raised. Allow time for the glue to dry completely. Have light blue construction paper and dark blue crayons. Remove the paper wrappers from the crayons.*
Peaceful Kingdom Collage: Have a long sheet of mural paper or a piece of poster board, pictures of animals, glue sticks, and markers.
Doves of Peace: Offer each child a piece of light blue construction paper and a dark blue crayon. Help the learners hold a piece of paper firmly on top of a dove outline and rub the side of a crayon back and forth over it. **Do you see a peaceful dove appear where you were rubbing? In the Bible, the dove is a sign of peace. Doves help us remember that God wants us to love others and live in peace.** Learners may want to make overlapping doves or a line of doves.

Peaceful Kingdom Collage: God wants the world to be a peaceful kingdom. Spread mural paper or poster board on the floor. Show the children the pictures of animals that you collected. Talk together about the animals and provide glue sticks for attaching the pictures to the paper. **Which animals might want to be together? Which might be afraid of each other? Some day all animals and all people will be friends.** Add trees, grass, water, and flowers.

Worship Together

M&P *Have a Bible, a leaflet, and the project from Kids Create above.*
Display the doves or the collage in the storytelling area. Open the Bible to the book of Isaiah. Read the key verse for this session: **"The wolf shall live with the lamb." Think about how frightened a lamb would be near a wolf. When God's peace comes, the lamb and the wolf will live as friends. God wants us to live as friends too. When we are kind, when we share, and when we show love for others, we are showing God's peace to others.** Make a peace circle by joining hands. Pray the prayer on the back of the leaflet.

Mary and the Angel

Session at a Glance	What You Need	What Learners Do
Ready for the Story (15 minutes)		
Welcome the Witnesses	• Baby dolls, blankets, diapers, bottles, infant toys	• Play with baby dolls.
Take a Look	• Birth announcements, envelopes	• Look at birth announcements.
Try This	• An adult visitor wearing angel clothing, white paper, marker	• Hear an important message.
Explore the Story (15 minutes)		
Story Set-Up	• Leaflet 14 (LR), glitter glue	• Decorate the angel who visited Mary.
Storytelling	• Bible, Leaflet 14 (LR), Poster K (TCK)	• Hear the story of the angel's visit to Mary.
I Can Too: Faith Traits	• Witness CD (TCK), CD player, "Little Book of Faith Traits" booklets (from Session 1), Sticker Sheet 1 (LR)	• Hear an angel song and add to their booklets.
Live the Story (30 minutes)		
Ways to Witness	• Small plastic yogurt lids, hole punch, photos of learners, scissors, yarn or narrow ribbon, glue, permanent marker	• Make a gift for family members.
Kids Create	• White construction paper, glue sticks, pieces of blue material (fabric, wrapping paper, ribbon, cellophane) • Strips of construction paper, tape, paper stars, yarn, marker	• Make an advent collage. • Make an advent chain.
Worship Together	• Bible, Witness CD (TCK), CD player, Leaflet 14 (LR)	• Thank God for the birth of Jesus.

14

Bible Text

Luke 1:26-56

Key Verse

Here am I, the servant of the Lord.
Luke 1:38a

BIG Idea

God works in the lives of people who are faithful.

LR = Learner Resource
TCK = Teacher Class Kit
M&P = Materials and Preparation

Teacher Prayer

Lord Jesus, we are waiting to celebrate your birth. Help us turn our hearts toward you. Keep us focused on the good news of your birth. Amen

Question for Reflection

Expectations about what must be done to get ready for Christmas may crowd out the important preparation of our hearts for Jesus. How can you make time for Jesus?

Learner Goals

KNOW

that an angel told Mary she would be Jesus' mother

GROW

in their trust that Jesus loves them

SHOW

love for members of their families

FACTOID

In Mary and Joseph's context, their families would have negotiated and contracted their engagement not as a personal, but as a familial and social, joining.

Bible Background

What Factors Shaped This Story?

Only the Gospels of Matthew and Luke tell the story of Jesus' birth and infancy. Luke tells of both Jesus' and his cousin John's births—each remarkable. John's mother Elizabeth was presumed barren and was "getting on in years" (1:7); Mary was a virgin. In other women, as well as Elizabeth and Mary, Luke emphasizes Jesus' inclusion of women as important.

What Is This Story About?

"Do not be afraid" echoes again and again in this Gospel, including from Jesus himself. We shouldn't be surprised that God's ways might seem frightening since they are so different from our own. Mary's response is not fear but perplexity and sensible doubt. "How can this be?"(verse 34) she asks when the angel tells her she will have a child. She wants an explanation. When the explanation comes that it is God's will she is ready and willing to serve. Mary's devotion and faithfulness reflect a motif in the Gospel of Luke.

Through the centuries, Mary's song has been sung daily in the church. Those denominations and religious groups that sing daily vespers include her song "The Magnificat," after the word that begins her song in the Latin translation. Note how clearly the song proclaims God's power for justice. The proud, the powerful, and the rich are dispersed in favor of those who fear God, the lowly, and the hungry. When the angel tells Mary, "Nothing will be impossible with God" (verse 37), the angel speaks not only of her pregnancy, but of the justice God promises.

The work of the Holy Spirit is another important emphasis in Luke and Acts, also written by the author of Luke. In this story the Holy Spirit bears the power of God (verse 35) and fills Elizabeth with the knowledge not only of Mary's pregnancy but also of its significance.

Why Is This Story Important?

Mary's pregnancy and call to serve are examples of what Luke's Gospel proclaims—that Jesus' mission is universal. His vocation is the salvation of the whole world, including, perhaps especially, those whom the world puts on the margins, for example, young women such as Mary. By the power of the Holy Spirit, God will through Jesus fulfill God's promise of justice and peace.

Age-Level Connection

Two- and three-year-olds may not have many Christmas memories. Help the learners hear that Advent is a time for "getting ready." What the church prepares for is the celebration of Jesus' birth. The children can join in the welcoming of the Christ child with singing, making things, and prayer.

Ready for the Story (15 minutes)

Welcome the Witnesses

M&P *Gather a variety of baby dolls, blankets, diapers, bottles, and infant toys.*

Be ready to greet the children at the door. **I'm so glad you're here to help us get ready.** Encourage the children to examine the dolls and baby items you gathered. **Who would like to feed one of the babies? Do you know how to put a diaper on one of the babies? Let's wrap the baby in a blanket to keep the baby warm. Are there babies in your home, or what other experiences have you had with babies lately?** Stay nearby to interact with the children and to encourage taking turns and sharing.

Take a Look

M&P *Locate or make several birth announcements. Place the cards in envelopes that the children can open.*

Bring the envelopes into the area where the children are playing. **Come see what I have. What do you think is inside each envelope?** *(Letter, birthday card, Christmas card.)* Have the children assist you in opening the envelopes and taking out the cards. **What do you see on the cards?** *(Babies or baby things.)* **These cards have a message about a new baby. Each card tells about a new baby that has been born.** Take time to tell the children the name or other details for each baby. **When a baby is born, the family wants everyone to know about this wonderful day. Today's Bible story is about a very special baby too.**

Try This

M&P *If possible, have an adult visit the class as an angel, wearing a white robe or an angel headpiece. Fold a piece of white paper in half. On the inside print, "Get ready! Get ready! Get ready for the baby!" Have the angel carry this message.*

Have your visitor knock on the door. Invite her or him into the room. **We have a visitor! Look at this person. Is this person wearing something special?** Comment on the robe or the headpiece. **I wonder if this person is an angel. In the Bible, God sends angels to give people important messages.** Ask the guest: **Do you have an important message for us?** Open the message and read the words to the children: **"Get ready! Get ready! Get ready for the baby!" I wonder who this baby might be. Can you guess?**

Witness WORDS

Mary, angel, Jesus

FACTOID

Angel is the Greek word for "messenger," though angels are often ascribed other roles. Gabriel is, along with Michael, the most prominent angel in biblical tradition.

Transition Tip

Have some children take the visitor to the storytelling area and explain some of the TCK items on display.

Explore the Story (15 minutes)

Kid Connect

When a baby comes, family and friends often bring gifts for the baby. Talk with the children about things that a baby needs. Prepare a note asking families to bring a gift for a baby to class next week. Locate a food pantry, shelter, or other organization that serves families with babies and learn what types of items they need.

More Movement

Encourage the children to think about how to get ready for a baby. Some things that people might do are put together a crib, buy a rocking chair, wash clothes, and go shopping. Act out ways of preparing for the arrival of a baby.

Story Set-Up

M&P *Have Leaflet 14 from each Ages 2-3 Learner Resource (LR), and glitter glue available.*
Hand out the leaflets and look together at the front page. **The woman who is wearing blue is Mary. One day an angel came to visit Mary. Mary was very surprised. Mary did not know why the angel came to her. The angel said, "Don't be afraid. I have good news for you." The angel had a message from God. We don't know just what angels look like but let's add something to these angels to make them sparkle.** Help the children apply glitter glue to their angels.

Storytelling

M&P *Have a Bible, one Leaflet 14, and Poster K from the Age 2–Grade 4 Teacher Class Kit (TCK) handy.*
Gather the children in the storytelling area. Open the Bible to Luke 1 and point to the story. **Here the Bible tells us about a time when an angel came to visit Mary. Listen to what the angel told Mary.** Read the story inside the leaflet. After the story, give the children an opportunity to respond to what they heard. Point to the picture of Mary on Poster K and remind learners of the people God called: Gideon, Samuel, Mary—and the learners. **God has important jobs for each one of us.**

I Can Too: FAITH|raits

M&P *You will need the "Little Book of Faith Traits" booklet (see page 9) and the Session 14 sticker from Sticker Sheet 1 (LR) for each child. Locate a CD player and the Witness CD (TCK).*
We know that after baby Jesus was born, a sky full of angels sang about him. Maybe this one angel who visited Mary sang too. Play the song "I Bring You Good News," Track 14 on the Witness CD. Encourage the children to try singing or humming along.

Distribute the "Little Book of Faith Traits" booklets and the Session 14 sticker from each Sticker Sheet 2. **The Faith Trait for today is patience. Mary waited patiently to hear what the angel said, and then she waited patiently for Jesus to be born. We need to wait patiently to celebrate Jesus' birthday, too, on Christmas.** Help put the stickers on page 14 and read the activity suggestion on the page. Collect the booklets to use next time.

Live the Story (30 minutes)

Ways to Witness

M&P *Use a hole punch to make a hole near the edge of a small plastic yogurt lid for each child. Cut yarn or narrow ribbon into 12" (30 cm) lengths, and trim photos of the children (see page 70) to fit the lids. Locate glue and a marker. Make a sample.*

In church we call this time for waiting, Advent. One way we get ready for Christmas is to show love for the people in our family. Show the children the sample ornament you made. Help them thread a length of yarn or narrow ribbon through the hole in a lid. Tie the ends to form a loop. Glue the trimmed photo to the lid. Print the child's name and the year on the back. **Hang these ornaments at home.**

Kids Create

M&P *Blue Collage: Gather white construction paper, glue sticks, a marker, and pieces of blue items such as fabric, wrapping paper, ribbon, and cellophane.*

Advent Chain: Count the nights until Christmas Day; cut a 1" x 6" (2.5 cm x 15 cm) strip of construction paper for each night for each child. Cut a 6" (15 cm) paper star for each learner and print this verse on each one: "Each night after prayers are said, take off one ring and hop into bed. When only the star is left to shine, you will know it is Christmas time!" Locate tape and yarn.

Blue Collage: During Advent the church wears the color blue. You can make a blue collage to help you wait at home. Hand out white paper. Spread out the collection of blue items. Provide glue sticks for attaching the pieces to the paper. **What are some things your families are doing to get ready for Christmas?** *(Accept responses.)* **Singing songs, praying, and reading the Bible are other ways.** On each paper print, "Blue is the color of Advent."

Advent Chain: Do you like to wait? What are some times when you have to wait? *(Accept responses.)* **We can make a chain to help us wait for Christmas.** Hand out strips. Show how to make a circle by bringing the two ends of the strip together and taping. Learners will need help and may finish their chains at home. Poke a hole near the bottom of the star and connect it to the chain with a piece of yarn. Explain how the chain will work.

Worship Together

M&P *Have a Bible, a leaflet, the Witness CD, and a CD player.*

Gather together and open the Bible to Luke 1. Read the key verse: **"Here am I, the servant of the Lord." When the angel came to Mary, Mary was happy. She was happy to be Jesus' mother and God's helper. We can be helpers, too, when we do things for people in our family, for our friends, and for people who need help.** Play the song "I Bring You Good News" on the CD again and then pray the prayer on the back of the leaflet. Point out the Advent wreath inside and suggest that families use it to count the weeks in Advent.

Teacher Boost

Take a moment to think about all that these children have learned about God's love from your ready smile.

Witnesses in the World

Your group can show love for needy babies by bringing things babies need to Sunday school next time. Together, generate a list of items such as diapers, formula, cereal, powder, baby wipes, and toys. Give each child a note about the gifts for babies your class will collect in the next session. Call families who are not present today.

GREAT good byes

At the door, offer a good-bye hug or handshake. **Help your families get ready for Christmas by displaying your collage or hanging your chain.**

Jesus Is Born

15

Bible Text
Luke 2:1-20

Key Verse
You will find a child wrapped in bands of cloth and lying in a manger. Luke 2:12b

BIG Idea
Jesus is for everyone.

LR = Learner Resource
TCK = Teacher Class Kit
M&P = Materials and Preparation

Session at a Glance	What You Need	What Learners Do
Explore the Story (15 minutes)		
Welcome the Witnesses	• Christmas decorations, nativity sets, shoe boxes	• Examine the figures of Mary, Joseph, and Jesus.
Take a Look	• Star ginger cookies, frosting, spreading tools	• Make gingerbread stars.
Try This	• The church sanctuary	• Take a Christmas walk.
Explore the Story (15 minutes)		
Story Set-Up	• Poster B (TCK), Leaflet 15 (LR), Sticker Sheet 2 (LR), crayons, Witness CD (TCK), CD player	• Follow the road to Bethlehem.
Storytelling	• Poster D (TCK), Bible, Leaflet 15 (LR), Witness CD (TCK), CD player	• Hear the story of Jesus' birth
I Can Too: Faith Traits	• "Little Book of Faith Traits" booklets (from Session 1), Sticker Sheet 1 (LR)	• Talk about joy and complete their booklets.
Live the Story (30 minutes)		
Ways to Witness	• Wrapping paper, tape, ribbon, baby gifts	• Wrap gifts for babies.
Kids Create	• White bags, newspaper, doilies, construction paper, scissors, markers, tape, glue, yarn, chenille craft stems • Blue construction paper, cotton balls, glue, star stickers, paper, scissors	• Make Christmas angels. • Make sheep of Bethlehem.
Worship Together	• Bible, cookies, juice, cups, doll, doll blanket	• Celebrate the birth of Jesus.

Bible Background

What Factors Shaped This Story?

The Roman Emperor Augustus ruled from 27 B.C.E. to 14 C.E. At the time of Jesus' birth, Palestine had been under Roman occupation for about 100 years. The Roman government exploited the people, who hoped for a leader who would bring justice and peace. "The world" referred to in verse 1 is the Roman empire. The Gospel writer Luke is both historian and preacher. Luke is intent on locating the story of salvation amidst specific times, places, and events of history. Salvation is God at work in history; history is the realm of God's activity.

What Is This Story About?

In a corner of a colony of the Roman empire comes the birth of a child. While emperor and military governor exercise power, an engaged couple travel, despite her pregnancy, to obey the emperor's decree. While world events transpire, God's messengers visit shepherds in their fields. The birth of the Savior comes in a specific historical time and place to turn the world upside down. The focus is on angels rather than on an emperor, on God's messengers rather than on imperial decree, on a newborn child rather than on obedience to the colonial power, on a manger in a stable in a small town rather than on a palace or grand house in a capital city. In the Roman world, the emperor was understood to be God's designated leader. Indeed, the emperor was himself considered divine. For Luke, the new child whose birth proclaims peace is God's chosen leader, "the Messiah" or *Christ*, which means "anointed."

Why Is This Story Important?

The center of world events is not necessarily Rome or Jerusalem or any world capital or other seat of worldly power. The center of world events is where God is bringing peace and salvation for all people. God's actions are not remote. Heaven and earth are not far from one another. Angels from heaven speak to shepherds in the fields. The Messiah is a human child.

Age-Level Connection

Young children are likely to know babies. They may understand that the arrival of a baby is a happy experience for most families. In this session you help the children share the joy of Mary and Joseph as you celebrate Christ's birth. At Christmas we are happy, too, because Jesus loves us.

Teacher Prayer

Lord Jesus, you came to earth as a child like the children I teach. Increase my love for you so that I see you reflected in each of the learners. Fill this time we spend together with happiness and joy. Amen

Question for Reflection

Christ came to earth in a way that mirrors the experience of every human being. How does knowing that Jesus came for everyone influence your thinking about situations in your community and in the world?

Learner Goals

KNOW
that Jesus was born as a baby

GROW
in their understanding that Jesus came for all people

SHOW
love for other babies

FACTOID

The "registration" that took Mary and Joseph to Bethlehem was a census required for purposes of taxation and conscription into military service.

Ready for the Story (15 minutes)

Witness WORDS

Bethlehem, manger, peace

Welcome the Witnesses

M&P *Decorate the room with Christmas items such as a small tree, pictures of Jesus' birth, and hanging stars. Locate one or more nativity sets that the children may handle. Bring shoe boxes to use as stables.*

Greet the children with: **Happy Christmas!** Point out some of the items you have added to your room. **Has anyone ever wished you a happy birthday? Christmas is Jesus' birthday.** Invite the learners to greet others with the phrases "Happy Christmas" or "Happy Birthday." Direct the children to the place where you have displayed the nativity sets. **Does anyone know who these people are? Here are Mary, Joseph, and Jesus.** Demonstrate how to move the figures into the stable and let the children play carefully with the sets.

FACTOID

Bethlehem, six miles (9.6 kilometers) south of Jerusalem, is King David's birthplace. Jesus' birth fulfills Micah's prophecy (Micah 5:2-4) that a new king will come from there.

Take a Look

M&P *Make or purchase star-shaped ginger cookies and some frosting. Have spreading equipment the children will be able to use easily (knives or craft sticks, for example). Before serving any food, check with caregivers for any learners with allergies. Provide an alternative, if necessary.*

Gather the children together and get ready to decorate star-shaped ginger cookies by washing hands. As the children work, encourage them to smell the Christmasy smell of the ginger. **What cookies or other special Christmas foods have you made with your families?** Save the treat for the end of the session celebration.

Try This

M&P *Plan to walk to the sanctuary to see the Christmas decorations. Consider having a few extra adults along.*

Sit together in the storytelling area. Greet the children again with: **Happy Christmas! Does anyone remember the story about Mary and the angel? What was the message that the angel brought to Mary?** *(She would have a baby. The baby would be Jesus.)* **When it was time for Mary to have her baby, she and Joseph walked to a town named Bethlehem. It was a long walk. Mary and Joseph were very tired when they came to Bethlehem. Let's pretend that we are walking to Bethlehem just like Mary and Joseph.** Walk as a group to the sanctuary, taking care not to disturb worship if it is going on.

In the sanctuary look at Christmas decorations. Help the children notice any special candles, flowers, banners, or other reminders of Christ's birth. **Christmas is a happy time. In church we remember that Jesus was born at Christmas time. God sent Jesus to us so that we could learn about God's love for us.** Walk together back to the classroom.

Transition Tip

As you return to the class area, walk around the room and then settle down at the table. Talk about how tired you are. **Mary and Joseph were glad to be in Bethlehem, but they needed a place to rest.**

Explore the Story (15 minutes)

Story Set-Up

M&P *Display Poster B (TCK). Have available Leaflet 15 from the Ages 2-3 Learner Resource (LR), the Session 15 stickers from each Sticker Sheet 2 (LR), crayons, the Witness CD (TCK), and a CD player.*
Look together at Poster B and talk about things the children and families are doing. **Are these homes and stores like ones near you? Which of these children would you like to play with?** *(Accept all responses.)* Explain that Mary and Joseph lived in a town like this.

Have helpers offer everyone a leaflet and a crayon. **What do you see?** *(A road, people walking, a town, moon and stars.)* **Mary and Joseph walked from their home to Bethlehem. They knew something important would happen there.** Listen to the song, "Jesus Is Born! Let's Celebrate!" on the Witness CD (Track 15). **Use your crayon to follow the road to Bethlehem.** Play the song as children work. Offer help if needed. Look inside the leaflets and help learners attach the baby sticker in the manger, the sheep sticker by the shepherd, and the music-notes sticker by the angel.

Kid Connect

Jesus was born in a barn in Bethlehem. It might have been cold and dark. Do the children know where they were born? Probably in hospitals and homes—clean, light, and warm places with doctors and nurses close by. Family members held and kissed and loved the children, just as Jesus' family did.

Storytelling

M&P *Display Poster D (TCK) in the storytelling area. Have available a Bible, one Leaflet 15, a CD player, and the Witness CD.*
Move to the storytelling area. Open the Bible to Luke 2. **Mary and Joseph went to Bethlehem with many other people. They were very tired. When they came to the town, there was no place for them to rest. They knocked on the doors of houses and hotels. No one had room for Mary and Joseph.** Encourage the children to listen, and join in actions like walking and rocking the baby, as you read the story inside the leaflet. **Look at the poster. What can you tell about the place where Jesus was born?** *(Accept all responses.)* Play Track 17, "Creature Sounds," on the Witness CD and talk about the animals baby Jesus might have heard that night.

More Movement

Pretend to be the shepherds with your sheep. Encourage the children to put heads down and go to sleep. Sing a Christmas song, or play one on a CD, and have them imagine that an angel is singing. Repeat the process of sleeping and waking again.

I Can Too: FAITH|raits

M&P *Locate the "Little Book of Faith Traits" booklets (see page 9) and the Session 15 sticker from Sticker Sheet 1 (LR) for each child.*
The Faith Trait for today is joy. Who was joyful in the story? *(Accept all answers. Everyone was joyful.)* Christmas is a time of year when everyone is joyful because God has come to us. Hand out the booklets and the Session 15 stickers to attach to page 15. Comment on the day's activity and then page back through the booklets. **We have learned about many Faith Traits, haven't we? You have learned a lot at church. Let's sing our "Spread the Good News" song with the words "I'll learn at church."** The song was introduced on page 9. The booklets will go home today.

Live the Story (30 minutes)

Ways to Witness

M&P *Gather wrapping paper, tape, and ribbon or yarn. Display the baby gifts children have brought in (see Witnesses in the World, page 75).*
When Jesus was born, people brought him gifts. We can give gifts to babies who need food to eat, diapers and clothing to wear, and toys to play with. Look at these wonderful gifts you brought in to share. What are they and how are they used? *(Accept all responses.)* Provide paper, tape, and ribbon or yarn for wrapping the gifts. Encourage the children's efforts.

Kids Create

M&P *Paper Bag Angels: You will need white lunch bags, newspaper, paper doilies cut in half, markers, transparent tape, glue, yarn, and chenille craft stems. Cut a 6" (15 cm) construction paper circle for each child.*
Sheep of Bethlehem: Set out blue construction paper, cotton balls, star stickers, and glue. Cut a simple 4" x 4" (10 cm x 10 cm) paper angel shape for each child.

Paper Bag Angels: An angel came to Mary with a message and angels sang about baby Jesus. Let's make Christmas angels. Give each child a white lunch bag to open. Crumple pieces of newspaper to fill the bags and tape them shut. Demonstrate how to cut paper doilies in half and glue one half to the back near the top of the bag. Provide construction paper circles for faces. Use markers to make facial features. Glue the face near the top of the bag and add yarn hair and a sparkly chenille craft stem halo. **Your angels can sit near your beds to be with you while you sleep.**

Sheep of Bethlehem: What animals heard the news about Jesus from the angels? *(Sheep.)* **What did the angel say?** *(A baby is born. His name is Jesus. God wants peace on earth.)* Provide sheets of blue construction paper and white cotton balls. Show the children how to glue the cotton near the bottom. Distribute star stickers and the paper angels for the sky. **Imagine how the shepherds felt that night as they watched their sheep!**

Worship Together

M&P *Set out a Bible, cookies, juice, and cups. Before serving any food, check with caregivers for any learners who have allergies. Provide an alternative, if necessary. Have a baby doll wrapped in a blanket (or invite a parent to bring a baby to visit).*
Sit together at the table. Distribute napkins and cups. Show the children the cookies and juice, and thank God for this special snack to share at Christmastime. When everything is cleared away, introduce the baby or show the doll. Talk about babies and the baby Jesus. Open the Bible to Luke 2 and read the key verse: **"You will find a child wrapped in bands of cloth and lying in a manger." Jesus was born for you,** *(insert each child's name).* **God sent Jesus to everyone because God loves us so much.**

Teacher Boost

Jesus came into the world to show God's love for us. Each week you share that love. Looking into the children's eyes and listening to what they have to say does so much to show them that you value them as individuals.

Witnesses in the World

People all over the world celebrate the birth of Christ. If possible, bring in a book with pictures of Christmas celebrations around the world. Encourage the children to look for pictures that interest them.

Go Global!

Read the Go Global! activity on Reproducible Sheets S and T (TCK). See page 3.

GREAT good byes

Gather leaflets and other projects to go home. If you have a small gift for the children, hand them to the learners at the door. Offer a hug or a handshake to each child as he or she leaves. Share Christmas greetings with families and caregivers.

Bonus Sessions

What Are Bonus Sessions?

The five Bonus sessions during each semester of Witness offer theme-based learning opportunities in a shorter, particularly flexible format. Bonus sessions provide additional content for Sunday school programs that need more than 15 sessions per semester. They can also be used when teachers want experiential learning with a different pace.

What Is the Content of Bonus Sessions?

Bonus sessions offer the same set of categories represented by different Bible stories in each semester. In the **Jesus' Teachings** category, learners take a look at one or more of Jesus' teachings. Learners make **Old Testament/New Testament Connections** when they compare and contrast related Old and New Testament texts. Each semester, learners can take a **Field Trip** to explore a space outside of the classroom. A **Seasonal Preparations** session is offered each semester to provide an additional session on Advent (Semester 1) or Lent (Semester 2). Bonus sessions in the **Worship** category provide a time for learners to investigate faith practices and worship styles.

When Should I Use Bonus Sessions?

Bonus sessions can be plugged into the schedule at any time. If you have one, the Sunday school coordinator should coordinate group plans, especially related to Seasonal Preparations. Ask your Sunday school planner if Bonus sessions across age and grade levels will be planned for the same day, or if you have flexibility in scheduling them. If you are doing your own planning, browse through the Bonus sessions to see which ones you'd like to use and when.

What Are the Parts of a Bonus Session?

The first page of each Bonus session gets teachers and kids ready to learn. Pre-class preparation helps for the teacher, and one or more Ready for the Story activities for kids launch the Bible story investigations. The second page provides Explore the Story and Live the Story options for digging into the Bible story and making life applications. Some of the same sidebar headings from Core sessions are included in Bonus sessions.

What Do Learners Use during Bonus Sessions?

The learner resource for the Bonus sessions has two parts, neither of which is part of the Core learner resource. Each Bonus session has one reproducible page printed in the teacher guide and one reproducible sheet found in the teacher class kit. Be sure to make arrangements for timely and efficient photocopying of the appropriate pages and sheets for your group.

Vine and Branches

Bible Text

John 15:1-17

Key Verse

I am the vine, you are the branches. Those who abide in me and I in them bear much fruit. John 15:5

BIG Idea

We are connected to God and each other.

M&P

READY FOR THE STORY

Gather together a basket, leaves with stems, a black permanent marker, green floral tape, and a long flexible stick.

Bible Background

John 14–17 is Jesus' farewell speech. Jesus leaves a legacy and gives instruction for life after his death. Jesus talks about our relationship to him and to God the Father, to one another, and to the world. Then he prays for himself, his immediate disciples, and the whole church.

The vine and branches are one image of how we as believers are together in Christ. Visualize a vine and its branches. See how the vine and the branches together make the plant. Abiding in Christ the vine we abide in relationship with one another. When Jesus says that "apart from me you can do nothing" (verse 5), he is also talking about our relationships to one another. A branch cut off from the vine and apart from other branches cannot survive. The vine is an image also for Jesus' words (verses 3, 7) and love (verses 9-10), which also bear and sustain us together. Abiding in Jesus' words and God's love we live, thrive, and bear fruit.

As branches are sustained on a vine, we are sustained in Christ. As branches are one plant sprouted from and joined on a vine, in Christ we are born and joined together. Christ is love, nurtures and sustains us with love, and bequeaths love to us for loving one another. As Christ the vine sustains us in love, so we sustain one another. Our lives are joyful (verse 11) when we live mindful of this reality.

Ready for the Story (15 minutes)

Connected by Faith: As the learners enter the room, welcome them by name and direct them to the basket of leaves. Ask each of them to select one favorite leaf. Help them print their names on their leaves with the marker. **How would you describe your leaf?** *(Color, size, shape, smell.)* **Where did your leaf come from?** *(Vine, tree.)* **What makes a leaf grow?** *(Rain, sun.)* Explain that leaves must be attached to the vine or branch for them to get what they need to grow. If they separate from the vine or branch they dry up and die.

Show the learners the stick. **Jesus is like the vine that the leaves grow on. Through faith, we are attached to Jesus like the leaves are to the vine.** Ask the learners to show their leaves with their names on them. Use the green floral tape to wrap the learners' leaves onto the stick. Display the newly made "vine" where it can be easily observed.

Explore the Story (15 minutes)

Nourished by God: Scatter leaves under the unrolled shelf paper on a worktable or the floor, and help children feel where the leaves are. **Jesus said, "I am the vine, you are the branches."** Demonstrate how to hold a leaf firmly under the paper and rub the paper above it with the side of a crayon. Invite learners to make several rubbings each, filling the paper.

A vine brings water to the leaves to help them grow. Jesus, the vine, makes a way for God's love to get to us. Without this life connection, we wouldn't grow. Look at the paper of leaf rubbings. Together, draw a vine that connects with every leaf. After the vine is complete, point out that everyone is connected to each other too. **Jesus expects us to love and care for each other.**

Pass out Repro Page A and help each learner match up the leaves.

Live the Story (30 minutes)

A Living Vine: Sit all together in a circle. Hold on to the loose end of the yarn, and roll the ball to a learner. This learner holds on to the yarn where he or she catches it and rolls the ball to another learner. Continue until the yarn is gone and the "vine" has been well established with learners having had it passed to them more than once. **Jesus teaches us that we are all connected to each other. We stay attached to Jesus and God by hanging on to the vine. If we let go then we are no longer able to receive this gift and we won't grow in God's love. The Faith Trait for today is cooperation. Jesus' friends work together, play together, and cooperate because they love one another.**

Beauty on the Vine: Distribute paper and sponge shapes to learners. **Because we are joined together with Jesus on the vine, we grow and are made beautiful by God.** Put a small amount of glue on the small plates. Show how to press the sponge leaves into the glue on the plates and stamp the shapes onto the heavyweight paper. Sprinkle the glue print with glitter. Draw a glue-vine connecting the leaves with glitter glue.

Hand out copies of Reproducible Sheet I. The V is for Vine activity can be adapted so that hearts can be added to these beautiful vine pictures.

Closing Prayer: Thank you for our friends, dear God, and for our time together. Thanks for teaching us to care for ourselves and for each other. Amen

M&P

EXPLORE THE STORY

Have an assortment of leaves, crayons with paper wrappings removed, and a roll of lightweight shelf paper. Make copies of Repro Page A (page 92).

LIVE THE STORY

Have available a ball of green yarn. You will also need heavyweight paper, sponges cut in leaf shapes, white glue, glitter glue, small plates, and glitter (green and other colors). Make copies of Reproducible Sheet I (TCK).

Learner Goals

KNOW
together through Jesus

GROW
in their understanding of God's love for all people

SHOW
this relationship by being considerate of each other

Teacher Prayer

Dear God, through your Son, Jesus, the stories of your love and commitment to us are made clear. Guide my teaching so that I may pass your stories on to those in my care. Amen

Question for Reflection

The story describes Jesus as the vine that nourishes us with God's Word. A leaf cannot be reconnected to the vine. But if we let go of the vine, and later realize our mistake, can we be reconnected to God?

Bread of Life

Bible Text

Exodus 16:1-16; John 6:22-35

Key Verse

For the bread of God is that which comes down from heaven and gives life to the world. John 6:33

BIG Idea

God gives us everything we need.

M&P

READY FOR THE STORY

Put a formal place setting, including a place mat, plate, cup, knife, fork, spoon, and napkin, in the middle of the group table. Make copies of Repro Page B (page 93). Locate crayons.

Bible Background

The people crossing the sea (John 6:22-24) recall the ancient people's crossing the sea to freedom (Exodus 14:21-24). In the desert, God provided food: manna or bread from heaven, and water. God provided enough for everyone—not too much or too little. Earlier in John 6, Jesus fed thousands of people, making enough from one boy's five barley loaves and two fish.

People responded to Jesus being able to feed so many people. Anyone who has the resources to feed a hungry multitude can command an audience. In fact, the crowd sought to make Jesus king (John 6:15), not only that his power would provide food for them but also that his power might liberate them from Roman occupation as Moses had liberated the people from Egyptian slavery. People expected these things of the promised Messiah.

Jesus points beyond the food that fills bellies to the food that endures and sustains life. Yet that divine food, he says, "comes down from heaven and gives life to the world" (John 6:33). Heaven and earth are joined in that food. God's work and human work are joined, and God's work is in believers' believing and following Jesus.

Jesus stands in the traditions of the people, continues those traditions, and does something new. He is both like Moses and different from Moses. He not only gives bread but also is himself bread, not earthly food, but relationship with Jesus who was sent from heaven to the world. As God provided food in the wilderness for the people, God provides food for us in our need. God feeds and nourishes not only our bodies but our whole selves. In Jesus, God gives us the Bread of life.

Ready for the Story (15 minutes)

Ready to Eat: As the learners enter the room, greet them warmly by name and guide them to a place at the table. **What do you see here?** *(A place mat, plate, cup, knife, fork, spoon, and napkin.)* **How does it feel to sit down to a table set for a meal but without food?** *(Accept responses.)* **Long ago in Bible times, God's people the Israelites were hungry. They had walked and walked in the desert after escaping from danger. But they needed food! Guess who gave them the food they needed.** *(God.)*

Distribute Repro Page B and have children find and color the loaves of bread.

Explore the Story (15 minutes)

Take What You Need: Pass the empty basket among the learners. **The Israelites' baskets were empty and they were complaining because they were hungry. Then God said to Moses, "I am going to rain bread from heaven for you, and each day the people shall go out and gather enough for that day." God told the Israelites to take as much bread as they could eat but no more. So they went out with their baskets and gathered manna—a kind of bread—brought it back to their tents, and shared it with their families.**

Invite the learners go out into the room with the empty basket, and gather the "bread" (pieces of white paper) that was left for them. **Did you find all that you need? Is there enough for each person?** Have them exchange paper pieces for the crackers, and enjoy a snack after thanking God for all good food.

Pass out copies of Reproducible Sheet J and talk about some of the projects to do at home. Note especially the "Bird Food Basket."

Live the Story (30 minutes)

Bread from Heaven: Reread John 6:33: **For the bread of God is that which comes down from heaven and gives life to the world.** Have the learners form small loaves from playdough and place the loaves on small paper plates to dry. Use a marker to add the learner's name and a title like "God's Bread" or "Bread of Life" to the plate. The loaves may be painted after they have dried thoroughly. Pass out Repro Page B to each learner. Complete now or at home.

No One Goes Hungry: God wants everyone to have enough to eat. Jesus even said, "I am the bread of life." Use the cookie cutter to cut one or more cross shapes from a slice of bread. **The crosses remind us of Jesus and his love for us. Let's share God's gift of bread with our friends**.

As you eat, note any other crosses in your room. **The Faith Trait for today is reverence, so remember to fold your hands and thank God for this bread—and all of the good things God gives us. What are some others?** *(Accept all responses.)*

Closing Prayer:

Thank you for the bread we eat.
Thank you for the friends we meet.
Thank you for our time today
to be with friends at church and play. Amen

M&P

EXPLORE THE STORY

Have several crackers for each child, and a basket. Cut or tear white paper into pieces, several for each child, and hide them around the room. Before serving any food, always check with caregivers for learners who have food allergies. Provide an alternative, if necessary. Make copies of Reproducible Sheet J (TCK).

LIVE THE STORY

Have playdough, small paper plates, a marker, paint (optional), sliced bread, and a cross-shaped cookie cutter. Before serving any food, always check with caregivers for learners who have food allergies. Provide an alternative, if necessary.

Learner Goals

KNOW
that God provides for them

GROW
in their trust in God

SHOW
this trust by sharing with their peers

Teacher Prayer

Dear God, please give me patience so that I may trust in you. Amen

Question for Reflection

Was it a surprise that the Israelites hoarded the bread from heaven, which could have stopped as suddenly as it had started?

The Sacrament of Baptism

Bible Text

Romans 6:1-11; Acts 2:37-42

Key Verse

Repent, and be baptized every one of you in the name of Jesus Christ so that your sins may be forgiven; and you will receive the gift of the Holy Spirit. Acts 2:38

BIG Idea

Baptism welcomes us into God's family.

M&P

READY FOR THE STORY

Have available several plastic bowls or pans partially filled with water, plastic cups, kitchen sponges cut in shell shapes, and large shells. Have towels for cleanup.

Bible Background

Baptism is the rite of initiation into the Christian community. Various religions include rites of purification and initiation, including washing with water. As a Christian sacrament, Holy Baptism is a means of God's grace with an outward sign (water) and God's promise of our salvation as children of God. Christians today don't always agree about what age baptism is appropriate; what, if anything, is required; and the physical method of baptizing.

Paul taught that God's salvation was for all who believe. Believers receive salvation in Christ by being united with Christ in Holy Baptism. This means being united not only with his life, but also with his death and new life. Believers are free from sin and death. This doesn't mean that believers no longer sin or die. It means that sin and death no longer exercise power over believers who are free to live new lives and not to sin.

Romans and Acts emphasize changing one's mind and life in response to belief in Jesus Christ. Baptism conveys the forgiveness of sins and the gift of the Holy Spirit who empowers believers for life in Christian community. Being members of the Christian community and followers of Jesus Christ make a difference in one's life. Believers' lives are devoted to the "apostles' teaching and fellowship, to the breaking of bread and the prayers" (Acts 2:42).

Scripture teaches us the practice of baptism but witnesses a variety of teaching and practice regarding Holy Baptism. At the center of Holy Baptism is a life-transforming relationship with God in Christ Jesus: we are united with Jesus and freed from sin and death. Freed and forgiven, we can live our lives devoted to God and to one another.

Ready for the Story (15 minutes)

Washing with Water: As learners arrive, welcome them individually and invite them to the area for water play. **What can you do with water?** *(Drop things into it, try to float them, scoop water from one bowl to another.)* Supervise some exploration. **Water is fun and it's also an important part of the baptism service. When we are baptized, we are washed clean and we are made part of God's family.** Allow some time for drying off.

Explore the Story (15 minutes)

Baptism Action Rhyme: Baptism—becoming a member of God's family—is a happy occasion. Today's Faith Trait is harmony, sweet sounds and movements that remind us we are part of God's beautiful creation.

We are baptized in the name of God the Father, Jesus the Son, and the Holy Spirit. Hand out Repro Page C for children to complete. Note the three clouds. Introduce the words and actions to the baptism action rhyme.

Water falls upon my head. *(Point to head.)*
1, 2, 3 *(Point to fingers, 1, 2, 3.)*
"In God's name," Jesus said. *(Hold hands together in prayer.)*
1, 2, 3 *(Point to fingers, 1, 2, 3.)*
With this water I'm baptized. *(Cup hands as if holding water.)*
1, 2, 3 *(Point to fingers, 1, 2, 3.)*
I am special in God's eyes. *(Point to eyes.)*
1, 2, 3 *(Point to fingers, 1, 2, 3.)*

Live the Story (30 minutes)

Welcome to God's Family: When families receive new members, they celebrate. Joining God's family is something to celebrate! What word do families use when they want to tell someone they are glad to see them? *(Welcome.)* **Today we will make welcome signs to hang in our homes for our families to see.**

Pass out cardboard with the invisible message "Welcome to God's Family" in raised glue letters. Secure lightweight paper over each dried message and show how to rub with the side of a crayon. The message will appear. Decorate and display at home.

The "Welcoming God's Family" activity on Reproducible Sheet K would be an appropriate follow-up to this activity, to do now or encourage families to do at home.

Baptized in God's Name: Make a brief visit to the baptismal font in your worship space and let children touch the water. **All of God's children, young and old, are invited to be baptized and join the family of God.**

Return to the classroom and provide each learner with a piece of construction paper and three blue water-drop shapes. Help the learners glue the shapes on their paper and add the numbers *1, 2, 3.* Print along the bottom of each child's page, "_____ is God's child."

Be sensitive to those who may not be baptized. Assure them that God loves all of them. You might suggest that parents or guardians of unbaptized children talk with the pastor about baptism.

Closing Prayer: Thank you, God, for my place in your family. Thank you for loving me always. Amen

M&P

EXPLORE THE STORY
Make copies of Repro Page C (page 94).

LIVE THE STORY
Use white glue to print "Welcome to God's Family" on light cardboard for each learner; dry it thoroughly. Gather lightweight paper, masking tape, and crayons without wrappers removed. Make copies of Reproducible Sheet K (TCK). Arrange a visit to the baptismal font. Have available construction paper, three blue paper water-drop shapes per learner, glue, and a marker.

Learner Goals

KNOW
that God calls them to be baptized

GROW
in their understanding of what baptism is

SHOW
that they are members of God's family

Teacher Prayer

Dear God, thank you for inviting me to be a part of your family. Support me and share your love with the youngest members of that same family. Amen

Question for Reflection

Is baptism like a "get in free" card to God's family for children and adults—or can it be revoked?

The Word Becomes Flesh

Bible Text

John 1:1-18

Key Verse

The true light, which enlightens everyone, was coming into the world. John 1:9

BIG Idea

Jesus is God's Word of love to all people.

M&P

READY FOR THE STORY

Locate a baby doll, wrap it in a blanket, and put it in a manger or box. Make copies of Repro Page D (page 95). Have crayons ready.

Bible Background

The Gospel of John celebrates the incarnation. God's divine Word becomes flesh. The mystery of Jesus is that he is both human and divine, earthly and heavenly, mortal and eternal. This Gospel was written "so that you may come to believe that Jesus is the Messiah, the Son of God, and that through believing you may have life in his name" (John 20:31). Believers are beckoned to partake of the divine life Jesus brings to us.

As God spoke the cosmos into being (Genesis 1), again God speaks and God's Word becomes flesh. That Word—Jesus—is God's self-expression. That Word—Jesus—is eternal and always with God and, at the same time, coming into the world, into history, with us. That Word—Jesus—is the true light and enlightens everyone. By him, believers may witness and share in the divine life as God's own children born of God.

John, too, was sent from God as a witness to what he had not yet seen. None of us has seen God, which might make believing in God hard, except that God's Word in the human Jesus makes God known.

In the ancient Greek world God and human, spirit and flesh, and heaven and earth were sharply divided. In Jesus we meet God and human in one, signaling God's reconciliation with human beings. God's redemption in Jesus Christ reunites spirit and flesh. Heaven and earth meet in Jesus. We can live together with God.

Ready for the Story (15 minutes)

Baby Jesus: Greet the learners by name as they enter the room, and guide them to the baby in a manger scene you recreated. Encourage them to pick up the baby and see how it is wrapped in swaddling clothes. **Who do you think this could be? What do you know about the birth of Jesus? Who sent Jesus to live with the people on earth? What does it mean to make a promise? God's Word was given that Jesus would be born. Is that what happened?**

Continue passing the baby around carefully until each child has had a turn holding it. **Today's Faith Trait is patience, a word that gives us hope. God promises good things like new babies, and gives us the patience to wait for them. Remember that God keeps promises!** Hand out Repro Page D and crayons so everyone can draw baby Jesus.

Explore the Story (15 minutes)

God's Word: In the beginning there was nothing. Not one single thing. God's Word created everything. On the table in front of us are examples of things that are part of God's creation. Invite the learners to pick up the items and look at them closely. **What do you see? What colors are they? What do they feel like? Describe the items. How are they the same? How are they different?** *(Accept all answers.)* **Can you think of anything else that is here because of God's Word?** *(Oceans, mountains, fruit, vegetables, stars, people!)*

Sing the "Spread the Good News" song introduced on page 9. Name all of the items and others the learners think of, using the song pattern on page 10 ("God made trees.").

Live the Story (30 minutes)

"John Says" Game: Play a variation on Simon Says with the learners. **The Bible tells us that God sent a man named John to get people ready for Jesus. Whenever I say, "John says" to do something, do it. Whenever I say, "John says, 'God made you' or 'Jesus loves you,'" clap your hands and cheer.** Include actions like *jump, stand on tiptoes, wave hands,* and *smile.*

A Light in the Darkness: Have you ever been worried because it was dark? What did you do? With Jesus we never have to fear the darkness. Pass out heavyweight paper and paintbrushes. Set out glow-in-the-dark paint and help learners paint a large cross in the center of the paper and then decorate all around it. Once the paint dries, the picture can be put on the wall or hung on the ceiling over a bed. **After some exposure to light, the cross will glow brightly in the dark, and remind you that Jesus us always with you.** The "Star Light" activity on Reproducible Sheet L also involves the use of some glow-in-the-dark materials. Hand out those sheets to go home.

Closing Prayer:

Thank you for your baby Son.
You sent him so we'd see
How much Jesus means to you,
And how much that means to me. Amen

M&P

EXPLORE THE STORY
Gather a variety of nature items, such as leaves, rocks, dirt, a feather, a flower, and a carrot.

EXPLORE THE STORY
Have out heavyweight paper, paintbrushes, glow-in-the-dark craft paint, and copies of Reproducible Sheet L (TCK).

Learner Goals

KNOW
that God's Word is a promise

GROW
in their understanding that God keeps promises

SHOW
that they can tell God's good news to others

Teacher Prayer

Dear God, you keep your promises. Please grant me the courage to keep my own promises to my family and those in my care. Amen

Question for Reflection

God keeps all promises. There are no exceptions. Why, then, is it so difficult for us to do the same?

A Place to Pray

Bible Text

Luke 11:1-13

Key Verse

So I say to you, Ask, and it will be given you; search, and you will find; knock, and the door will be opened for you. Luke 11:9

BIG Idea

Jesus teaches us how to pray.

M&P

READY FOR THE STORY

Cut 9" x 6" (23 cm x 15 cm) pieces of construction paper. Have crayons and scissors available.

Bible Background

The Bible frequently tells of Jesus praying. Increasingly surrounded by people eager to hear him, Jesus sometimes went alone to pray (Luke 5:16; 9:18). Having engaged in controversies and conflicts with the religious leaders, Jesus might pray through the night (Luke 6:12). Jesus prayed with others as part of corporate worship and he prayed with his disciples (Luke 9:28). As Jesus was facing his death, he prayed (Luke 22:41-42). Jesus prayed from the cross (Luke 23:34). Jesus' final words were words of prayer (Luke 23:46). Seeing that prayer was such an important part of Jesus' life, it's not surprising that his disciples asked him to teach them to pray.

Jesus' response to the disciples has four parts. Jesus teaches them a specific prayer (verses 2-4). Jesus teaches the importance of persistence in prayer by comparing how God responds to their prayers to how a friend might respond even to an inconvenient request (verses 5-8). Jesus teaches by giving words of encouragement to pray—ask, search, knock—and reassurance that prayers receive responses (verses 9-10). Jesus teaches that God's response to their needs expressed in prayer is like a good parent's response to a child's needs (verses 11-13). The Bible has two versions of the Lord's Prayer (Luke 11:2-4; Matthew 6:9-13). Ancient manuscripts have additional variations. Protestant church traditions add a doxology, words giving glory to God, which are based on David's prayer in 1 Chronicles 29:11-13.

When we talk and listen to God in prayer, we acknowledge that God is a friend who is ready not only to listen to our prayers, but also to respond. Practice helps us know that we can always go to God with the words and feelings of our hearts and minds. The prayer Jesus taught gives us words to use alone or with others. (Notice, though, that the prayer uses "us," "our," and "we," drawing us to one another as well as to God.) We can use the Lord's Prayer anytime, perhaps especially when we aren't sure what to pray or can't find words to express what we want to say. Jesus encourages us both to persist in prayer and to trust God's loving response.

Ready for the Story (20 minutes)

Prayerful Hands: Greet learners by name and remind them to greet each other. Guide them to the work table where they will find the supplies for tracing around their hands. Help trace around their open hands with little fingers next to each other. Fold the paper in half (folding the hands together) and cut around the hand shape, keeping as much of the fold intact as possible. Decorate. **What do we do with our hands in church?** *(Accept all answers.)* **Jesus taught his friends and us a special prayer. Let's pray the prayer together out loud. How do we place our hands when we pray?** Ask learners to demonstrate balancing their cut-out hands on their real hands and holding them together. Then pray.

Today's Faith Trait is self-discipline. Seeing these paper hands and feeling them together can remind your "self" to pray every day.

Explore the Story (20 minutes)

Prayer Sewing Cards: Each Sunday in church we pray the prayer that Jesus taught us, called the Lord's Prayer. Jesus teaches us to ask and it will be given to us; seek and we will find; knock and the door will be opened. Pass out the pairs of church shapes. Stack the two shapes, then give each learner a length of yarn and help them sew the sides of the churches together. Cut up the middle of the top church, open it, and glue the copy of the Lord's Prayer to the inside. **Your prayer sewing card can remind you to pray Jesus' prayer at home too.** Some learners may complete Repro Page E while you help others with the sewing cards.

Live the Story (20 minutes)

We Pray Together: Jesus taught those who followed him a prayer to pray so that they could pray together as well as alone. Where is a good place to pray? *(At church, at the table, in bed, at Sunday school.)* **We can pray when we are alone, with our families, our friends or at church.** Give each learner a drawing of the church. Demonstrate how to use a finger and washable-ink stamp pad to make fingerprints all around, inside and out, of the drawing. Then show how to use the markers to turn the prints into people praying at church.

Prayer Place Mat: Jesus reminds us to thank God for the blessings that we receive. Name a time during the day when we should stop and thank God for our gifts. *(Lunch, dinner, bed time all times.)* **Do you pray before you eat? What prayers do you say?** Pass out the sheets of construction paper, the drawings of your church, and the copies of the Lord's Prayer. Help learners glue the prayer onto the larger paper. After they add more color to their place mats with crayons, carefully seal with clear adhesive paper. **Put your place mat at your place at the table to remind you to thank God for gifts of family and food.**

Reproducible Sheet M has an activity (Saying Prayers) that involves drawing something kids are thankful for on a paper plate. You might coordinate that project with this one, or suggest that families do it at home.

Closing Prayer: Thank you, God, for listening to my quiet prayers. I feel so loved and safe, just knowing that you're there. Amen

M&P

EXPLORE THE STORY

For each learner, cut two matching simple shapes of a church from an old file folder, and a copy of the Lord's Prayer to fit on the church. Punch holes along the left and right sides of each cutout. Make copies of Repro Page E (page 96)

LIVE THE STORY

Make a simple line drawing of your church for each child, and have washable stamp pads, fine-tip markers, and wet wipes for cleanup. Also have for each child a piece of 12" x 18" (30 cm x 45 cm) construction paper, a line drawing of your church, and a copy of the Lord's Prayer. Gather crayons, clear adhesive paper, and glue. Make copies of Reproducible Sheet M (TCK).

Learner Goals

KNOW

that Jesus teaches us how to pray

GROW

in their understanding of what a prayer is

SHOW

that they can say their own prayer of thanks

Teacher Prayer

Dear God, guide me to teach others how to seek you in prayer. Amen

Question for Reflection

Prayer is a powerful tool. Is one person's heartfelt prayer as powerful in God's eyes as a prayer prayed by a group of people?

Vine and Branches

John 15:1-17

Like leaves on a vine, we are connected to Jesus.
Draw a line between the leaves that match.

Bread of Life

Exodus 16:1-16; John 6:22-35

God gives us bread so our tummies feel full. God gives us love so our hearts feel full.
God gives us everything we need. Draw a line around the loaves of bread.
How many did you find? __________

The Sacrament of Baptism

Romans 6:1-11, Acts 2:37-42

We are baptized in the name of God the Father, Jesus the Son, and the Holy Spirit.
Count the hearts and draw lines connecting them. What is in the middle?
Use a blue crayon to add drops of water.

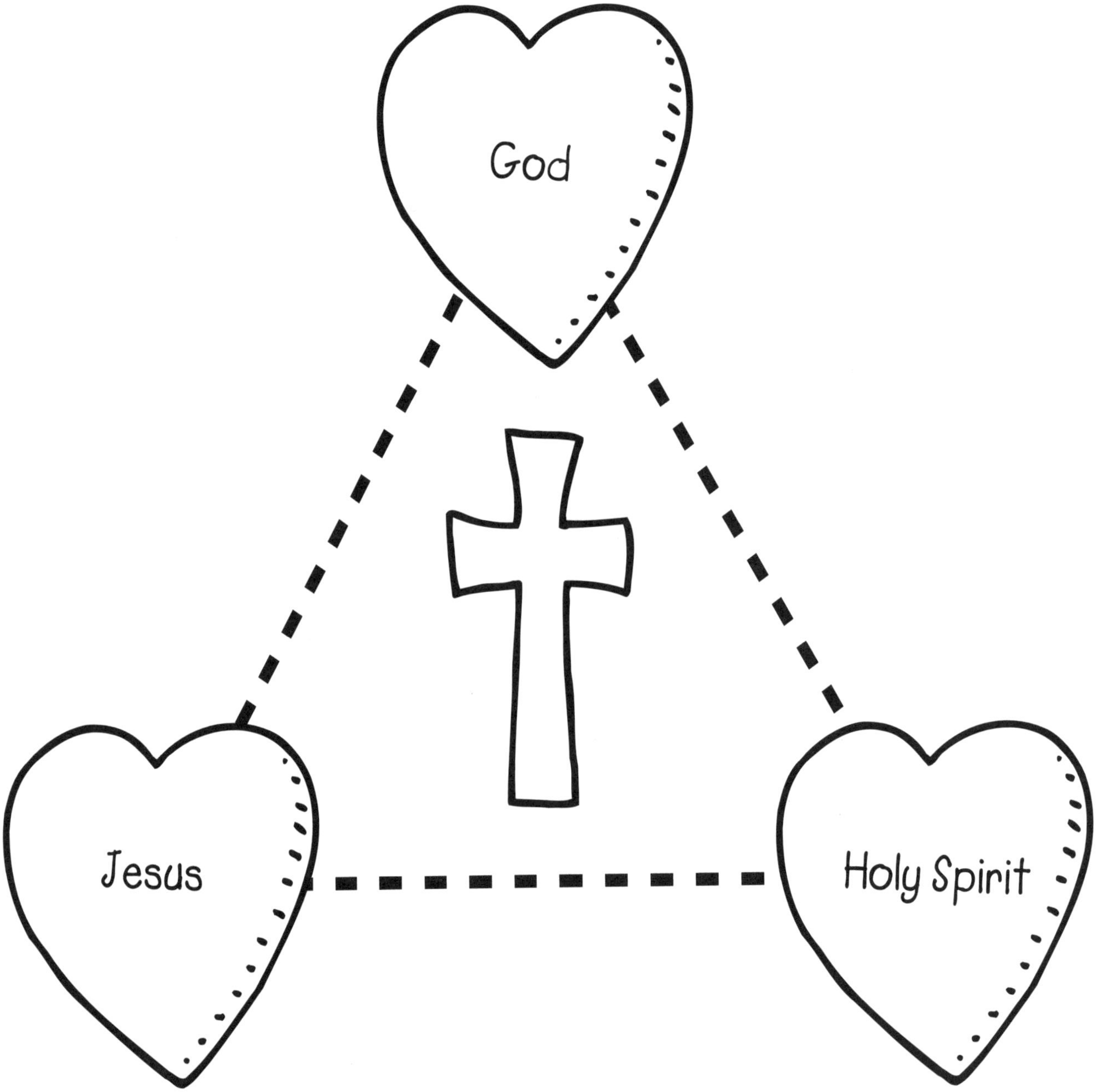

The Word Becomes Flesh

John 1:1-18

God became a person and lived on earth.
That person was Jesus, the baby we celebrate at Christmas.
Draw the face of baby Jesus and color his blanket.

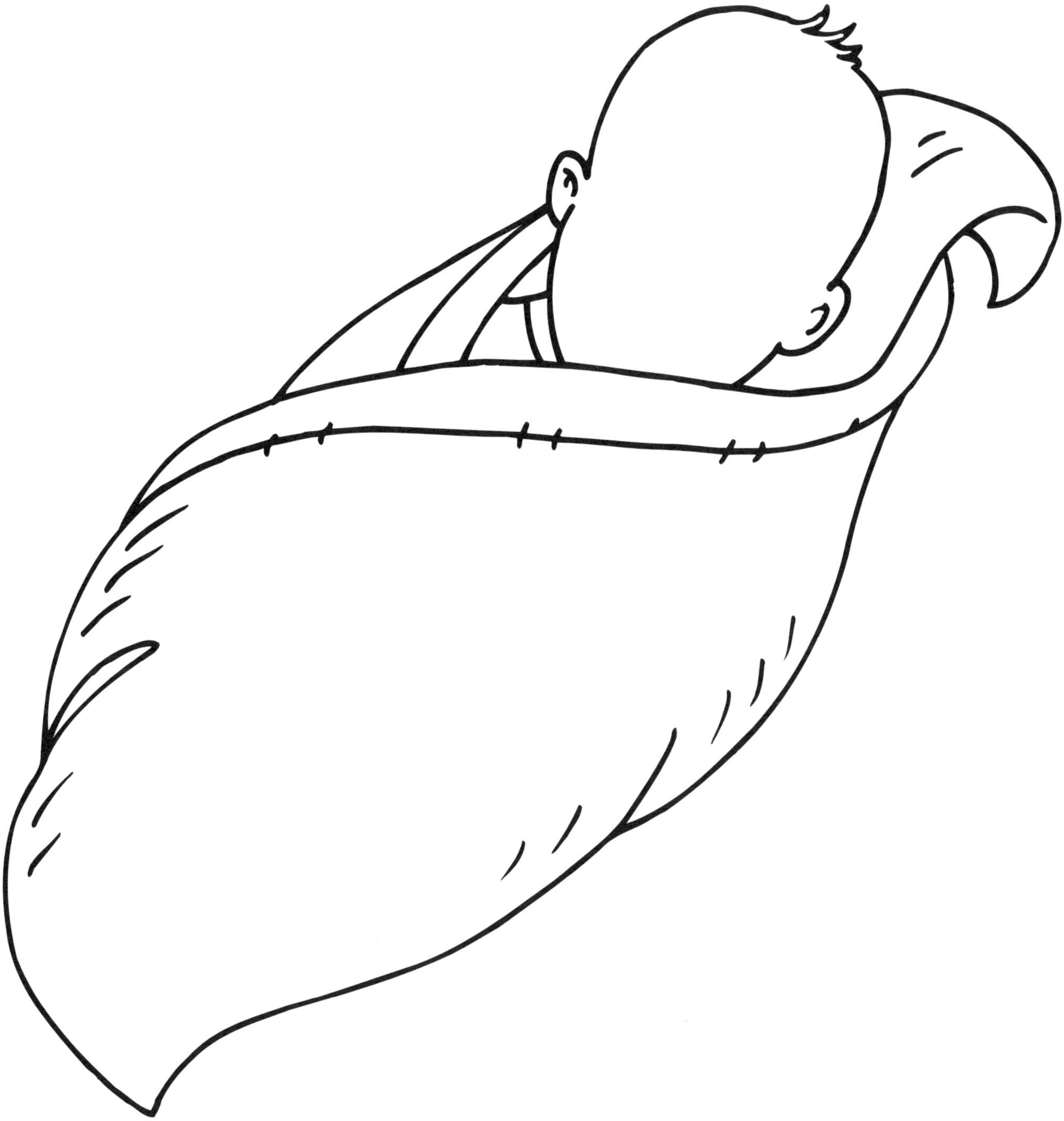

A Place to Pray

Luke 11:1-13

Jesus taught us how to pray. We can pray together at church.
Find and color the four church crosses. Color the rest of the picture too.